The Catholic Company Man

The Catholic Company Man

Collisions of Faith, Catechism, and Company Meetings

Eric M. Meyer

RESOURCE *Publications* • Eugene, Oregon

THE CATHOLIC COMPANY MAN
Collisions of Faith, Catechism, and Company Meetings

Copyright © 2022 Eric M. Meyer. All rights reserved. Except for brief quotations in critical publications or reviews, no part of this book may be reproduced in any manner without prior written permission from the publisher. Write: Permissions, Wipf and Stock Publishers, 199 W. 8th Ave., Suite 3, Eugene, OR 97401.

Resource Publications
An Imprint of Wipf and Stock Publishers
199 W. 8th Ave., Suite 3
Eugene, OR 97401

www.wipfandstock.com

PAPERBACK ISBN: 978-1-6667-4459-0
HARDCOVER ISBN: 978-1-6667-4460-6
EBOOK ISBN: 978-1-6667-4461-3

AUGUST 25, 2022 2:51 PM

"Never forget that there are only two philosophies to rule your life; the one of the cross, which starts with the fast and ends with the feast. The other of Satan, which starts with the feast and ends with the headache."

—FULTON SHEEN

Contents

Preface ix
Acknowledgements xv

1	The First Company Man	1
2	500 Beers and the Seminarian	10
3	Day One and a Dilemma	19
4	The Corporate Case for Faith	27
5	Ash Wednesday at the Sales Meeting	37
6	The Orthodox Cabbie	41
7	268 Slides	49
8	Waffle House	55
9	Purity and the Customer	61
10	A Cold Walk in Billings	67
11	Men's Room Confession	73
12	So Goes the Family, So Goes the World	80

13	Me Against the Lizard	86
14	Trashin' Hotel Rooms	98
15	Fired and Faith	108
16	So What Now?	115

Appendix   119
Bibliography   129
About the Author   131

Preface

Growing up, I had a fairly typical American faith experience. My family went to church every Sunday, the kids attended Catholic school, and everyone volunteered at the annual parish festival. We identified as Catholic. It was who we were as a family. And it was a large part of who I was as a person.

But the Catholic Church had an identity crisis in the seventies and eighties. The aftermath of the Second Vatican Council caused mass confusion. The church was marred by debate, and they lost my generation in the shuffle. A lack of good catechesis and overall enthusiasm for the faith left me wanting. For example, I attended the nondenominational youth groups like Young Life because it was "way cooler" than anything I could get at the local parish. Mass on Sundays. Young Life on Mondays. And so it went for the formative years of my life.

I never missed Mass. Even on vacation, my family was in Mass. Sure, my old man always preferred the "vacation option" when we were out of town. But my mom always fought it, and we would end up sitting in some church in Hilton Head, wondering why we flew across the country to sit through yet another boring Mass.

I knew there was something special about the Catholic faith. I knew the Eucharist was different, something Catholics only had, but beyond that, my knowledge was limited.

Here's a simple example of powerful theology I never knew. Check out this quote:

> "And from that day forward up until today, this has been an uninterrupted chain: they baptized their children, and their children

Preface

their own, and those children . . . And also today this chain continues."[1]

That little ditty is from Pope Francis's homily on the Feast of the Baptism of the Lord.

Christ was baptized to set an example from which we, in our filthy humanity, have followed *unbroken* for two thousand years? Why didn't somebody tell me that information! All those years, I just thought it was a nice ritual to symbolize the gift of the Holy Spirit or something. I had no idea I was on the hook to *not break the chain*—holy moly!

Could I have been taught all this theology and forgotten it? Could it have gone in one ear and out the other when I was young and stupid? It's possible. I blame only myself for my lack of knowledge about the Catholic faith. But I do think that we can go deeper and understand our faith further. I think that the adults in the church should educate the younger generations in a deeper understanding of the faith. The chain has not broken for two millennia. For it to remain unbroken, we need to step up the religious education and instill in our children an understanding of the importance of the Catholic faith.

Preserving the unbroken chain—that is why an under-qualified, never-published, non-theologian, corporate middle manager wrote this book.

* * *

The hope is that this book is an on-ramp for guys like me who are willing to take a deeper look at the faith in which we were raised. If you're anything like me, your faith experience went something like this: You attended Mass at a neighborhood parish. Sometimes you paid attention, most of the time you didn't. Your dad still attends church there. Heck, you may have gotten married there. You went to grade school at the local parochial school. You volunteered at the fall festival every year. It was a big deal. You don't remember what you gave up for Lent during those years, but you do remember how good the fish fries were. Overall, you had the typical American Catholic experience.

Nobody pressed me on the hard questions of faith. Nobody ever asked if I understood that this church I begrudgingly attended every Sunday is the oldest continuously operating organization in the world. How did that happen? How in the world did an organization *that* boring string together

---

1. Pope Francis, "Feast of the Baptism of the Lord", para. 1.

Preface

a two-thousand-year run that included an unbroken line of 266 leaders? For starters, it's not actually boring at all. I just thought it was. And you probably did, too.

I hope that somehow this book finds its way to other guys like me. In a way, I've written this book to myself, the guy who grew up in the faith, still goes to church, but never thought all that hard about it along the way. I pray that you, reader, will grow more curious about the faith and subsequently begin a deeper understanding of it.

To do that, I'm going to reach you where you're at: corporate America. We're taking God to work. Chapter by chapter, I will tell my corporate tales and then go a little deeper into how those experiences in corporate America shaped my faith walk and how you can be a strong man of faith in the corporate office. It's not easy, but it is doable.

My story is pretty typical of a cradle Catholic, as we're labeled. I grew up Catholic, went to Catholic school, and did the whole deal. I went through all my sacraments like any good boy. Memories of my first communion are as fresh as if it were yesterday. My parents gifted me a Boy Scout pocketknife and a brand new $2 bill on a beautiful spring Sunday morning. The US Mint started printing $2 bills back in the seventies, and everyone thought they were cool, or at least I did. The white suit I wore was awesome. That knife might even still be in my old tackle box.

Until high school, my memory serves that I was a pretty good kid. Even thereafter, I steered clear of jail or any long-term embarrassment. Drugs were not an issue. I didn't play in a metal band or knock up any cheerleaders. Partying wasn't really my thing, so I probably had a total of three beers and a couple of those Bartles & Jaymes wine coolers my entire high school career. It was the eighties, and I was just a typical kid who mostly stayed out of trouble while waiting for the next U2 album to hit the record shop.

Then came time for confirmation. I just wasn't all that interested. Deep theological objections were certainly not keeping me up at night. Pinpointing a reason is difficult. My mom was more upset than my old man at the idea I would forego confirmation. You see, my mother grew up in a devout German Catholic family in Cincinnati, Ohio. She was born in the forties and experienced the church when the Mass was in Latin. In those days, it was completely normal and expected that at least one member of the family would become a priest or a nun. She followed suit, broke up with the guy she was dating, and joined the convent after her senior year of high school.

Preface

Although very devout, my mother ultimately decided to leave the convent and marry the same guy she had sent packing a year earlier. That guy is my dad. They had a great marriage. I tell people at parties that my mom was a nun. It works for a good laugh.

Back to the story, I don't even remember why I was disenchanted about confirmation. After thinking it over for thirty-five years, I think it was worse than disenchantment. I was just bored.

About a year later, I went through confirmation with little fanfare, then got on with my life. My college years went by equally vested in the books and the beers. Okay, maybe it was more like 60/40 with the scales tipped toward the malted hops. I attended the University of Dayton in Ohio. All my college buddies were Catholic, and we never missed Mass. In fact, there was a 10:30 p.m. Sunday night option, and we were the regulars. Talk about a slacker Mass.

Over the years, my career developed, and marriage soon followed. I met my wife in a bar, and before too long, we had our first daughter. Then we had our second, third, and fourth. All girls. The Almighty had a plan for me to be a girl dad, which is a blessing that leaves me breathless every day.

It became obvious very quickly that my wife and I needed to figure out the moral ground on which we were going to raise the girls. She was a Lutheran, and I was a Catholic. I was adamant that our kids would be Catholic, but I'm not sure either of us really knew the difference between the Lutes and the Romans. She wasn't opposed to the notion of becoming Catholic, but nor was she impressed by my theological chops when I couldn't even answer the most basic questions.

My wife and kids are the ones who really brought me back to life in the church, and I am eternally grateful that God hung in there with me while I went from bored to curious yet clueless. My interest in Catholicism reenergized, and my career took off in parallel. Any company meeting would come with long nights in the bar and all the filthy chatter you might guess you would hear after eight beers in a Marriott lounge. The stories in this book come from those years. I wouldn't say I was living a double life, as the focus was always on faith and family, but for a long while it was necessary to check my Catholic worldview at the door in order to fit into the corporate mold. But the thing is, I've learned a lot from those years. The more I learn about the brilliance of the Catholic faith, the more I know we cannot go to church on Sunday and drop F-bombs the rest of the week.

Preface

God gave us free will. "God created man a rational being, conferring on him the dignity of a person who can initiate and control his own actions." (CCC 1730). That is well established in Scripture, but we seem to gloss over the fact that he also gives us the roadmap to follow him. He gives us the project documents and specs for living a good life, but he never forces alignment to the program. This is where we, as Catholic men, need to up our game. We need to know the parameters of the *Catechism*, which clearly line out how we are to live. This is the whole point. Either Christ established a church and way of life that is *everything*, or he was just a crackpot that the Romans hung on a tree. If the latter is true, we're clear to watch football on Sunday for nine hours. If the former is true . . . it's time to wake up.

If you are a cradle Catholic who goes to church and also goes through the motions, this book is for you. Our Catholic faith truly is incredible. Christ set it up to bring joy and fulfillment and peace to our lives. It is not for a second boring. Bishop Robert Barron said it perfectly in his book *Catholicism*: "Catholicism is a celebration, in words and imagery, of the God who takes infinite delight in bringing human beings to fullness of life."[2]

God gave us all the answers, literally. If we pay attention, we have been given the answers we need on politics, religion, sex, marriage, kids, economics, and the value of life itself. It's quite a travesty that somehow, in our flawed humanity, we ever got bored in the first place.

Heaven awaits. Read on.

---

2. Barron, *Catholicism*, 5.

Acknowledgements

In no particular order, I offer my sincere appreciation and thanks to those who bothered to engage and offer their honest take on this little project.

Daniel R. Hopkins — Editor

Gracjan Kraszewski — Guidance

Father Chase Hasenoehrl — Wisdom and example

Shannon Calloway — Review and input

Jason Calloway — Spelling police

Elizabeth Meyer — Sketches

Nicole Nadreau — Sketches

Bishop Danny Meagher — Review, historical context, and input

Regan Monnin — Review and input

Aaron Olanie — Review and input

Jim Becker — Review and input

Heather Meyer — Input, review, correction, love, sandwiches

THANK YOU all . . .

1

The First Company Man

THE apostles must have dominated the cocktail parties. They must have been magnanimous personalities who always showed up bigger than the moment. They could never have been normal dudes like you and me. Right? I mean, these are the guys who walk the halls at the national meeting like they own the joint. But perhaps we should look a little deeper.

Take a look at Peter the fisherman. He scammed the Romans, fished illegally, and fell deeply in debt. Profanity was very likely his first language. He knew how to hose brews, rip off dirty jokes, and wheel and deal. Then when the chips were down, he really blew it. He denied Christ three times but was man enough to ask forgiveness and fulfill his destined role in history. Without hesitation, Peter accepted Jesus' challenge to change the world. When it was all said and done, he accepted his crucifixion upside down so as not to disrespect the death of Christ.

That's just Peter. Paul, John, Andrew, and the others all lived their own incredible story. Each would have dominated reality TV today. Mike Rowe would make the story come alive on season five of *The Deadliest Catch*—"The Sea of Galilea."

Rowe: Pete. Now, you formed this little gang with no money and no real backing?

Peter: No, Jesus formed us, but he left me in charge after the damn Romans killed him.

Rowe: Wait, they killed your CEO?

Peter: Yep.

Rowe: A week after you showed up in Jerusalem?

Peter: Uh-huh.

Rowe: Wow. Are you going to throw in the towel? Go back to fishing?

Peter: Nope. They'll probably kill us before it's all over.

The ratings would have been off the charts. All told, the original twelve ended up being bigger than life, as each one played a major role in world history. Almost every one of them died a martyr. But they were nothing more than you and me at the beginning. They somehow knew their moment and when to act. If so, then my middle-management, twenty-year corporate run to the golden handcuffs may just be a starting point as well. Will I know how and when to act?

There are millions of guys grinding away at the job while still attempting some connection to our grand and magnificent Catholic faith. It's my story, but it's also the story of so many others simply because I'm not all that unique. Is a guy that works in finance at Xerox an apostle? Does being a middle manager at Boeing make you a candidate for sainthood? In this modern age, nobody is being stoned or hung on a cross in the break room for shooting their mouth off about God. At least not yet. Maybe we shouldn't be placed in the same group as Peter and John, but there is good to be done, and we must be the doers.

The biblical stories of the heroes and martyrs who literally built Christianity stone by stone are legendary. There are hundreds of incredible tales of ancient greatness. But there aren't many stories of Saint Bill from the Mailroom or Blessed Frank in IT. The apostles had jobs before they took on the world. They must have whined and moaned about the boss, the traffic, and the government just like you and me. But they just somehow figured out their exact calling at the exact right moment. Perhaps our sainthood awaits us if we can persevere in faith throughout careers littered with conference rooms, corporate travel, and meetings about meetings about meetings. The heroes, martyrs, and apostles didn't set a goal to acquire these labels. They lived the gospel in their everyday lives, likely never knowing the impact. Maybe our moment will come.

Vocation is a big word with a deep meaning. I never thought of my job in corporate America as a vocation. I can see how farmers and ranchers and miners can be satisfied at the end of the day because they literally give humanity the ingredients for life. Doctors can sleep at night, I would hope, since they fix broken people, and teachers must feel pretty good about molding young minds. But corporate guys, I don't know. There are a whole lot of seemingly endless meetings that can dilute any real feeling of accomplishment.

Even in the most efficient companies, the ones with the coolest products, there are guys who endlessly push PowerPoint presentations from conference room to conference room. I don't for a second question the value of what they do, but let's face it, not every job is glamorous. People get bored and go through the motions. Guys get lost while enduring decades of just getting by and providing for the family. Being a company man is noble, but it's really not all that sexy for 86.5 percent of us.

Is it possible that the day will come when corporate guys everywhere venerate Phil from Strategy & Communications as the patron saint of PowerPoint presentations?

* * *

Joseph of Arimathea might have been the first company man. Think about it. He shows up on the scene at perhaps the single most dramatic moment in history when he was the one chosen, according to all four Gospels, to deal with Jesus' body after the crucifixion. Take a second and think of that moment. The crowd is stunned. As Christ takes his last human breath, the moments following must have been the most awkward silence in human history. To the Romans, the two-bit rabble-rouser was no longer a problem. To the believers, the Romans had literally just killed God. Mary had to be shattered with grief beyond measure. Everyone must have just stood there in total shock with no iPhone to offer awkward rescue. Then in the middle of that silence comes a man, seemingly out of nowhere, to clean up the mess and bring some dignity to the moment.

Joseph of Arimathea is described as a wealthy disciple of Jesus, but he kept it on the down-low for fear of the Jews. Maybe he had the ancient version of a 401(k) and stock options from the startup he worked for in Jerusalem. There were no cell phones and pagers back then, but I bet he always rode on the newest model donkey, probably leased with an option to buy.

A respected man and member of the council, as it is written, suggests that Joseph was a mover and a shaker. He was in the know but kept his association with Christ separate. Sounds like a believer in the corporate world. Lay low. Do your job. Don't leave the coffee pot empty. Stay out of HR. Don't ever talk about religion. Could this guy be the first company man in recorded history?

Can you imagine the scene unfolding in the office that day?

"Boss?"

"What, Arimathea?" says the annoyed manager, short and to the point.

"Was just wondering if I could knock off a bit early. Just got a call on something personal."

"Sure, you have a tee time with Pilate, or what?"

"Not quite," Joseph nervously chuckles.

"Fine. But you better stay off the highway. Traffic is crazy. Evidently, they're crucifying some hothead downtown, and the crowds are huge. Nobody can find a parking place, and good luck getting an Uber out of downtown. Called himself king or something."

"Thanks for the tip," says Joseph as he sneaks out to play a crucial role in the history of Christianity.

Joseph and his counterpart, Nicodemus, ultimately worked a deal with the centurions who stood watch over the gruesome scene at the cross. They were authorized to take Jesus down from the cross after his brutal crucifixion. Once in their possession, they respectfully prepared the body for burial.

If you place this moment in the modern world, Joseph seems to be playing the director role while Nicodemus acts as project manager. Nicodemus seems to follow orders while his counterpart handles the leadership. Sounds typically corporate. Somebody has to take charge, or the whole project devolves into groupthink. Luckily, in this case Arimathea seems to have understood the magnitude of the situation, stood up, and called the shots.

Can you imagine if it took a corporate project group to get Jesus off the cross and buried? There would never have been an Easter Sunday. The project lead would have had multiple meetings about removing Christ from the cross. But then they would have had to get approval from three levels of management, which would have pushed the deadline out. A couple of missed emails and a permit that someone forgot to submit, and boom, we'd be celebrating Easter the next Wednesday. Anyone in a corporate role knows that groupthink is always lurking and waiting to derail any simple task. Easter Wednesday could have really happened.

Anyway, Joseph of Arimathea must have been a pretty good guy. Connected. He could hold his ground in the boardroom and still relate to the centurion guarding the parking garage. His buddies at the golf course probably called him "A-man" or "Big Joe." He likely knew how to operate in the big bad world and was pretty smooth.

As it turns out, he stepped up and played his God-given role well at the precise, right moment in history. I hope they can say that about me someday.

Just because the life and times of Jesus took place over two thousand years ago doesn't mean that the characters and circumstances were not relatable to our modern situations. The Bible is loaded with saints and sinners, righteous folks and trainwreck drunks, entrepreneurs and company men.

* * *

Matthias might be considered another company man found in the Bible. Chosen by Peter to replace the betrayer Judas, Matthias could be the first guy who actually had to interview for his role in the greatest story ever told.

Think about those fancy interview questions: "Tell me about a time when you cast out demons and fed the masses, then clearly articulate the precise steps you took in doing so, and demonstrate the measurable results." Give me a break.

Evidently, there's no mention of Matthias in the three synoptic Gospels, but in Acts it's noted that he had been with Jesus from his baptism by John and hung around all the way to the Ascension. So, here's a guy who's quiet, been there a long time, and by all accounts, a solid performer. Matthias is working away behind the scenes until there's an opening, and all of a sudden, he rockets onto the scene in the first chapter of Acts. How many times have you seen that scenario play out in a company setting? The discussion at the village water cooler probably went something like:

"Matthias? Matthias. Matthias . . ." says the guy racking his brain, trying to put the name to a face. "Is he that guy in accounting?"

"Mailroom."

"The guy with the long hair, long beard, and sandals? Wears the same tunic every day?"

"Yes. That guy. Promoted."

"Wow."

"Tell me about it."

"Did he even have to interview?"

"No idea. They probably just slotted him in . . . who is this guy anyway?"

"Brown noser, probably plays golf with Peter or something."

If we as members of the one true church are the body of Christ on earth, then I suppose it is predictable that we encounter situations similar to those the apostles faced all those centuries ago. The key to it all must be how we react and if anyone can sense in us a greater purpose. I know I was not the only believer working away in the corporate world, and there are people interested and willing to state the case for faith. But the corporate world can be cynical, material, and self-oriented. If we are to be the light for the world, we're going to need a few guys alongside us in the trenches.

Another big personality in the Bible is John the Baptist. Many called him the precursor to the Messiah, and by any standards, this guy was a wild man. John, a powerful and dynamic speaker, spoke up and called out the idiots. A company guy could easily see him in the corporate setting.

John would have played the role as the big thinker and the rabble-rouser that challenged every strategic rollout. He would have perhaps been the guy from the marketing agency that comes in with the orange skinny hipster pants and his hair all over the place. Everybody would know this guy and what he thought.

Turns out John the Baptist played his biblical role without fear and with absolute precision. He was the advance team for Jesus. He was market research and market shaping. John began his ministry as a very outspoken preacher who predicted the coming of the Messiah. Baptizing with water, he preached that someone much mightier than he was on the way and that people had better shape up. When the Roman ruler Herod entered into an unlawful marriage, John called it out publicly (Matt 14:1–12; Mark 6:17–18) and was imprisoned. He also demanded accountability of his own followers by requiring fasting and other disciplines. He walked the talk.

John the Baptist would be the guy in the conference room you would always be watching. On any given day, when the PowerPoint slides are stacked up by the hundreds and someone rolls out some "mission critical" initiative, John would be the one that sat and waited for the right moment. Then he upended the whole meeting by laying it all out on the carpet.

"Whoa . . . hold up. Go back two slides. I question the research here. Where is the need? Is it really wise to take the entire sales force off the job for a week of situational training?"

"Yes, we believe it is," responds the overpaid consultant.

Back to John. "Have we had any serious issues? Are cases in HR rising?"

"Not to date."

"Then why are we solving a problem we don't have?"

"To prevent one," the consultant drops his tried-and-true groupthink answer.

This John would never back down to the corporate "good idea fairy," and secretly everyone in the room loves him. Most corporate folks would never speak up or bring forth contrary opinion. It's too risky and too painful. By the time you get to the big-presentation-two-hundred-slide-PowerPoint phase, all decisions have been made, and no matter how much common sense is proposed, you will lose. Then you will be labeled as the guy who asks the stupid questions and prolongs meetings. But the beauty of John the Baptist is that he didn't care.

"Fine, but you just said we don't have a problem. If you take the sales force off the job, and we miss earnings, and we can't get back on track, then we'll have to lay everyone off. That will also solve it."

Silence from the overpaid consultant.

John the Baptist knew that Christ was coming. He knew the critical nature of the prework. Status quo and groupthink would be detrimental to progress. Someone needed to speak up and pave the way, and it would likely take pissing a few people off. John's story ends at the business end of a Roman centurion's blade, but such was the occupational hazard, given the magnitude of his role in history. God gave John the Baptist the necessary skills for his moment, and he nailed it. Perfectly.

* * *

My hunch is that the apostles were a lot like me and today there are millions of guys like me out there. We go to Mass every week but don't really know why. We are good, hard-working people by any measurement. But faith unfortunately falls more into a category of checking the box before the NFL game of the week.

We have to get back to the original value proposition of Christianity. God is loving. He sent his son to a hideous death to save us, and our redemption is predestined regardless of our own failings. There is such a thing as heaven and such a thing as hell. They are real. How we live matters. The proposition of Christianity is that we can literally be plucked out of the misery of humanity and given our own place in paradise.

It seems that since about the 1970s, the emphasis on heaven, hell, and solid teaching of the *Catechism* has given way to a catchy country song that says everyone wanna go to heaven, but nobody wanna go now.[1] Weekly visits to Mass didn't mean the ear was seeking knowledge (Proverbs 18:15). My old man taught me to work hard and save the hard-earned cash. He taught me how to be a man. But we never discussed and digested the origins of the faith and its critical elements. Now that I'm an adult, well into my career, I can see the need for more solid grounding in the *Catechism*. If that grounding existed for more Catholics, the world might well be in better shape.

According to the Pontifical Council for Justice and Peace, a 2014 document published by the Vatican on the vocation of work, the church beautifully sets up the case for faith in the company man:

> "When businesses and market economies function properly and focus on serving the common good, they contribute greatly to the material and even the spiritual well-being of society."[2]

Think about the last time you walked in a conference room to report that your company was contributing to the spiritual well-being of society. Most of the time, the AV doesn't hook up correctly, much less achieve perfect harmony between the task at hand and spiritual fulfillment. The world is tough because we are constantly juggling and struggling to find balance. It's good versus evil every day. Even the best of us are riding a seesaw that teeters between the natural inclination toward sin and the fact that every single human being is unique in their view of the world.

Coming to consensus in this life is tough. Making everyone actually happy is impossible. But going back to the statement above, if we can focus on serving the common good, we can greatly impact the material and spiritual well-being of our communities. Wait, so just like that, I go from

---

1. Chesney, *Lucky Old Sun*, "Everybody Wants to go to Heaven."
2. Pontifical Council for Justice and Peace. "Vocation of the Business Leader," 2.

thinking my corporate role isn't really impacting much to knowing I have a *vocation* to bring about some good.

My theory is this: if given a solid and perhaps a bit humorous on-ramp to study apologetics and theology, it just might be possible to reintroduce the absolute greatness of the Catholic faith to guys who haven't given it much thought. My own road back to Christ was too long but not too late. But I don't recall anyone reaching me, right where I was, in order to pull me up and out of the keg stands. The Catholic material I remember was either too vanilla and too touchy-feely or on the other end of the spectrum, well beyond my intellect and interest. When I was upside down on a keg, it was hardly the time for Aquinas.

Young Catholics need to be taught and challenged by their old man as well as by formal church education. It's got to be more than Sunday Mass. Kids need to see the faith being wrestled with and figured out by their parents. Proverbs 22:6 lays it out crystal clear: "Train the young in the way they should go; even when old, they will not swerve from it."

That puts me and you on the hook to know the faith and live it. If you are like me and thought Genesis was in the back of the Bible, it's time to kick it into gear before your daughters are piercing their noses and your sons are vaping in the back lot of the Arby's.

We can't teach or model what we don't know, so we must have a place to start that fits where we are on a subject. Anatomy first, then brain surgery. The overused "Jesus loves me" bit was always too simplistic for me. On the flip side, I couldn't track for five seconds with *Summa Theologica*.[3] There really wasn't much in the middle that could attract and draw me further out into the deeper theological water.

If you are anything like me, you cannot just dive into the deep end of the pool on any given subject. I need to start with rubber-band airplanes and then slowly work my way up to astrophysics. Let me put it more simply. Guys like me need to start with Pabst Blue Ribbon and work our way up to single malt Scotch. It takes a while to discover the good things in life. The good news is that we have all that we need waiting for us in the history and tradition of our great church. It's all there if we just read it.

---

3. St. Thomas Aquinas's famous writings were written between 1265 and 1272. He was canonized by Pope John XXII on July 18, 1323.

2

500 Beers and the Seminarian

My romance with medicine lasted six weeks. That's right. I attended the College of Osteopathic Medicine in Des Moines, Iowa, for less than sixty days.

There was a movie out at the time called *Gross Anatomy*. Everyone called me Slovak after the main character who struggled with med school. By the time the curtain fell, he sorted everything out, got the girl, and was on his way to a renowned proctology career. In my case, I felt like such a loser by quitting that I forced myself to take and pass at least one exam before pulling the ripcord. The facts are the facts: I didn't flunk out. I quit.

Then I joined a band of traveling buskers called Up With People. I rolled out of medical school right onto the tour bus in Tucson. It was 1990, and I was young and stupid. There were seventy-two women in the cast and thirty men. I couldn't sing or dance, but my odds were good. I'd never been in a choir, never done theater, never sang in a band. I didn't care. I was hooked.

My dad was a doctor. As the firstborn, I guess it seemed fitting to take the same route. But my dad never pressed me in any direction. I just wanted to be a good son, and deep down, he was merely waiting for me to step up and discern my own choices. With the med school decision finally concluded, he just quietly said, "I could see that coming, so figure out what to do next." I appreciate that short yet immensely understanding reaction more and more as I watch my own kids grow.

Conventional wisdom would label the med school dropout turned traveling busker as a questionable career move. My stock as marriage material dropped precipitously. The problem was I loved the vagabond gig. I caught the performance bug, and it has never let me go. Music was not my natural gifting, but I worked hard to train my two left feet. The 120 young people from eighteen different countries were far more experienced than me. There were guys and gals with real talent in this group. I didn't care. I sang in the harmony groups, tried out for dancing parts, and ultimately rose to MC of the whole show. Hard work paid off.

You may have actually heard of Up With People. It was a group formed in the sixties out of the hippie culture. The goal was, and still is, to build bridges of understanding between nations. It grew and grew, and by the time I jumped on the bus, UWP was the largest traveling production company in the world. Our show was a professionally produced variety show, and we played in big towns, small towns, and festivals all over the globe. The caravan came with buses, semi-trucks, and twenty tons of stage gear. There were five casts of over one hundred members on the road at any given time. We signed autographs and did press events. It was a very impressive troupe, and I was over the moon to be part of it all.

Our cast was called Cast C, and we drew the jackpot ticket. The tour booked gigs throughout the US, Mexico, Canada, and Australia. We performed in eighty-nine cities over the course of one year. That included an infamous pregame show at Super Bowl XXV that David Letterman mercilessly mocked on the Late Show.

So, what does this have to do with faith?

*　　*　　*

At this point in time, I was the top of my social game. I knew how to party, how to make the girls laugh, and could *really* put away the beer. The tour bus rolled on, town to town, seven days a week. Thus, getting to Mass was difficult, and frankly, I didn't miss it much.

The Catholic Company Man

That's me with the hat.

We flew to Australia immediately after the Super Bowl for a national tour. As the tour progressed, we sang and partied up and down Western Australia. We were a pretty big draw and got lots of attention town after town. Festivals, racetracks, beach towns, and outback villages were all dates on the tour shirt. The greatest show in my memory was in Canberra, the capital city. It was a festival called the Food and Wine Frolic. The locals called it the Alcoholic Frolic. The nickname lived up to the billing.

Our show was the afternoon set just before the headliner bands. So there we were, a family oriented hippie troupe singing songs of love and joy to twenty thousand inebriated Aussies. Dressed like *The Man From Snowy River*, in an oilskin riding coat and an Aussie cowboy hat, I took the stage for a timeless rendition of "Tie Me Kangaroo Down," Australia's most beloved nursery rhyme. Such was my fifteen minutes of fame, singing nursery rhymes to twenty thousand drunks. I'll never forget it. It was awesome.

After two months of total immersion in Australian culture, our last show was canceled. We suddenly found ourselves "Down Under" with one hundred of our best friends with two weeks to burn until our return flight to the US. Two weeks with nothing to do but party . . . in Australia? Watch out.

What would a band of international twenty-year-olds do with money and free time in Australia? You can imagine. We sprung into action, and about six of us rented a condo on the world famous Manly Beach and then proceeded to light the party torch. The goal was to drink five hundred beers in four days. We were idiots. Up With People was no religious organization, if you haven't gotten that sorted out yet.

About day three, my liver was beginning to wave the white flag. I was tracking near the top of the beer can leaderboard, but it was taking a toll. As the evidence piled up into a pyramid on the windowsill, I increasingly became aware that it was just too much. Finally, the third morning, I got up early after going to bed really late. People were sacked out all over the place. The only event on the agenda was stocking the fridge in advance of the push toward the summit, and that would not occur until well after lunch.

I laced up my jogging shoes, put my hat on backward, grabbed my $10 fake Ray-Bans, and hit the early morning streets. No shower. Hungover. Off to run away from everything. It was Sunday morning, mid-April 1991, and the Holy Spirit was about to physically grab me and speak to me.

* * *

All I wanted to do was sweat out the beer and forget about whatever embarrassing episode transpired the night prior. Jogging up through the neighborhood on the hill above Manly Beach, I heard church bells. The thought crossed my mind that going to Mass wouldn't be the worst idea in the world. I kept running. And finally found myself on the campus of what seemed like maybe a Catholic high school.

The bells continued to ring as I drew closer and closer. Foster's Lager continued to sweat through my pores while my head reminded me of how many cans I contributed to the pyramid. The school was scenic with its old brick buildings, and the bells kept ringing. I just ran.

Then, in perhaps the most galvanizing moment of my life to that point, I collided head-on into another person. I came around a corner of one of the buildings in full stride, and there was a guy, my age, robed in a cassock.

"Oops. Sorry," I said as I broke my stride.

"No worries, mate."

"Say, do you know when the Masses are today?"

I might as well have been Tommy Boy looking for the weight room.

"Yes. Now. Come with me."

"Yeah, no. I'm sweating like a hog. I'll come back later, cleaned up."

"No. Come with me."

The guy in the cassock may have actually grabbed me by the arm and pulled me along. I don't remember. Either way, I complied.

The next hour and a half was indescribable, but here goes. This guy, my age, is studying to be a priest. The place I've been running around and around is a seminary, and this guy leads me into their morning Mass. I found myself with twelve seminarians and one or two other civilians in a beautiful, serene, peaceful little chapel. All I could think was, "Holy crap, I must smell like beer. What am I doing here?"

Mass commenced, led by someone who I have come to believe was the lead priest of the seminary. It was beautiful. I don't remember a word that was said. I sat in awe of the contrast of it all. My life contrasted a million percent with the life these guys were discerning. It was such an intimate setting that there was no way I could blend in or be anonymous. It was just me, God, and twelve young apostles, and I was underdressed and smelled like a hangover.

Pope Francis talks about "smelling like the sheep," and in this case, that was me.

Then came the Liturgy of the Eucharist.

"Come with me," whispered my seminarian buddy.

"Huh?"

"Up to the altar."

Oh shit.

To this day, I don't recall if I was smart enough to even remove my ballcap, but there I was at the altar, participating in the Eucharist in my Jimmy Z bro-tank and Ray-Bans.

To coin a phrase from Genesis, I felt naked and afraid.

There must be something in the General Instruction of the Roman Missal[1] that says *do not* pull the hungover, sweaty, human disaster up to the altar. But there I was, fully exposed in my sin and filth. There was no cover. No place to hide. It seemed like these guys could see right through me and into that condo full of beer cans and passed-out twenty-somethings. At this point, I might as well be the other loser on the road to Damascus with Saul.

Conversion is not the correct way to classify that encounter, but it was *definitely* a wakeup call. I was caught in a moment. God grabbed me at the precise point where I was the farthest from him. Then I was physically carried home. More than thirty years later, I can feel that moment like it is still happening.

---

1. GIRM, as it is referred to, is the official procedural document of the US Conference of Catholic Bishops. The GIRM lines out every detail, requirement, and procedure of the structure of the Mass.

500 Beers and the Seminarian

I still wonder why that priest brought me up to the altar. I was a disrespectful disaster, or at least my clothing suggested as much. Anyone with an ounce of traditionalist in them would resoundingly say, "Get off the altar, and put some decent clothes on." I wasn't appropriately attired to be in the building, much less two feet away from the consecration. What a fool I was, but how beautiful the moment.

It was mesmerizing. I am convinced that my young seminarian friend was the Holy Spirit acting in human form.

I suppose as a side note to this scene, theologians could argue the pre-post Vatican II effects on dress code and decorum at Mass. I can only come to one, simple conclusion. The Holy Spirit was taking me, in all my filth, all the way to the cross. God was physically proving to me that the church is the hospital where I was to bring all the wounds caused by my sin. My state of readiness, proper dress, or cleanliness was immaterial to the magnitude of the moment.

I have never forgotten that morning. Immensely frightening, peaceful, and riveting, I just wish the story had a better ending. My only memory is jogging back to the condo and getting right back on the crazy wagon. I buried the whole experience deep in my heart. It took years to settle down, but that Mass was the only time I can remember actually being physically led back into the faith.

That seminarian may have saved my life. If he didn't actually save me, he certainly catalyzed the slow turn away from what could have been a couple more decades of ridiculous behavior. The Holy Spirit was clearly working on me, and I can honestly say that it was that one moment when I knew I had to change course. It was time to start growing up. I wonder what that priest is doing now?

* * *

As it turns out, the seminary was called Saint Patrick's Seminary in Manly. It has since been closed, and its successor is called the Seminary of the Good Shepherd. I was able to connect with Father Danny Meagher, who was a seminarian beginning at Saint Patrick's in 1989.[2]

By the simple deduction of the timing, Father Danny would have been there that day. He indicated that, in fact, a small group Mass of twelve would have been a group of seminarians in the same year of study.

2. Fr. Danny Meagher has since been appointed an Auxiliary Bishop of the Archdiocese of Sydney.

The only conclusion I can make from the limited information available from Father Meagher is that the group of men I was with that day were just like me. They were my age. We were all trying to determine what to do with our lives. They were facing the unknown. But while I was searching the bottom of beer cans and seeking the deeper meaning of Mötley Crüe songs, they were diving into the ancient truth of scripture.

The difference is that they somehow knew that God wanted them to be serious about their life. It took me a long time to figure that out, but that little miraculous collision was quite possibly the turning point.

* * *

What does draining beers and going to Mass hungover have to do with theology? A lot, when we finally acknowledge that the Holy Spirit is tugging at us in every circumstance.

Our *Catholic Catechism* has a lot to say about the Holy Spirit, and his entrance into the gospel story is a great one. Think of the state of the apostles at that moment. I mean, they had followed this guy Jesus who was a great, dynamic teacher. To put it in modern terms, this guy Jesus was the greatest keynote speaker in history. He made Tony Robbins look like a chump.

Jesus and his apostles had no venture capital, no sponsoring organization, no Under Armour endorsement, and no Instagram followers. They took out on foot all over the known world and sat down with people. They watched Jesus teach of a coming kingdom. They were awestruck as he fed thousands with a couple of fish, cured lepers, and brought people back to life.

Then just as their little startup was rolling into Jerusalem with a little fanfare and some corporate momentum, boom, their boss was brutally crucified. Game over.[3]

What were those twelve guys thinking? My money is on, "Holy shit, we're next." Then Jesus rose from the dead, and boom, game back on. But

---

3. The history of what was going on in the Roman Empire at the time of Jesus is fascinating. Jerusalem and the surrounding area was an outpost with a troubling Jewish uprising. Pilate was probably an up-and-comer in the military who was doing his time in a spot that wasn't all that glamourous. It was an incredible time for a nobody to show up, turn conventional thinking upside down, and change the world. That story is a book in itself. Rather than getting a PhD in history and spending decades diving into that subject, I offer you a quick yet excellent read. Grab a copy of *Killing Jesus* by Bill O'Reilly and Martin Dugard. They capture Jesus' moment in history brilliantly in a short, dynamic read.

within fifty days, Jesus had risen to heaven and left these twelve guys with the simple task of telling the whole world.

Can you imagine that conversation?

"Uh, hey, Andrew?"

"Yeah, Matthew?"

"What's your next move? Go back to fishing?"

"No idea. You?"

"Well, I can't exactly go back to collecting taxes. I think I burned that bridge," concludes Matthew with a bit of cynicism in his voice.

"What about this 'tell the whole world' bit?" James mouths off from the back corner of the apartment.

"Yeah, there's that," Andrew comes back with a heavy sigh.

"I wish he would have given us an agenda, a budget, some contacts, something."

"Wait . . . What a ride, fellas. I'm in. Let's go. We have what we need," Peter, the first pope, drops the leadership hammer just about the time the wind starts to blow through the apartment.

God shows up all over the Bible, associated with a mighty wind. The story of the Holy Spirit appears early in the book of Acts (Acts 2:2). When the apostles meet the Holy Spirit, he shows up as a fiery wind, which is reflective of a similar Old Testament scene where Yahweh descends on Mount Sinai during the Exodus (Exod 19:18).

One thing about the Bible is that the Old Testament almost always informs and sets up the New Testament. It is quite incredible to consider that thousands of years of handed-down stories, when there was no printing press and most people were illiterate, would come together brilliantly time after time.

The *Catechism* tells us how Jesus set up the Holy Spirit as the Paraclete. (CCC 692). Translated into our modern lingo, the Paraclete is our advocate or great counselor. In other words, Jesus has our back.

Let's boil it all down. Christ came, kicked off a movement, sacrificed his life, conquered death, and commanded the apostles to tell everyone and change the world. And here we are still talking about it two thousand years later. Christianity is, bottom line, the greatest startup in history, and we shouldn't be surprised when the Holy Spirit grabs us and asks us to participate. That's what happened to me that day Down Under.

From: Fr Danny Meagher (SGS) (External)

Sent: Wednesday, January 23, 2019 7:13 PM

To: Eric Meyer

Subject: Query

Dear Eric,

I am currently rector of the Seminary of the Good Shepherd, which is successor to St Patrick's Seminary, Manly, which you visited in 1991.

I was a seminarian then at St Patrick's, having begun in 1989. Fr Paul McCabe was the rector then, but I cannot tell from your email who the seminarian might have been who you met nor the group of seminarians you had Mass with. It seems that you joined a year group for the Mass, 12 being a normal group size back then. There would have been about 50 seminarians in all.

Sorry I can't be of more assistance.

God bless and its wonderful how the Holy Spirit can work in the most simple of ways,

Fr Danny Meagher

3

Day One and a Dilemma

THE guy in 10D just put his seat back into my knees and jarred me out of a most uncomfortable airplane nap. It seems fitting that a chapter on the struggle to remain faith-centered in the corporate world should begin with a jackass about 5'4" slamming his seat back on you from Newark to Seattle. For the record, I'm 6' 5". Whenever the short guy makes himself comfortable, it doesn't matter who you are, your first reaction is to unload the most creative profanity you know and rip the insensitive jerk's face off. Yet, somehow, we need to keep it together in this world. It's up to the faithful to be the guideposts.

After flying more than a million miles, there's not many places on the bucket list. At first, it seemed glamorous and even prestigious when I could report home all the stories and experiences. It didn't take too long before I'd been in every major US city, most of the best hotels, and about 80 percent of the Ruth's Chris Steak House chain. From sales calls in Thailand to meetings in Korea, filming a documentary in London and market research in LA, I'm grateful to have been involved in very interesting work. The problem is the glamour fades when all you want is to be home with your people.

The more interesting the project, the more I felt mismatched for the world. For example, I was in Wembley Stadium one night for a Tottenham Hotspurs match against Monaco. The whole place, all eighty thousand, was singing the Spurs' anthem. British soccer mayhem was on full display. My colleagues knew all the chants, and there were plenty of beers to go around. The experience of true English soccer is a bucket-list item. Yet all I wanted to do was go home. What was the matter with me? I'm sure I'm not the only one who feels this way. In fact, look around any airport as you travel for work or pleasure, and you can see the longing for home on the face of every road warrior.

The challenge of balancing work and home has offered valuable insight over the years. I understand now why there is a long tradition of unmarried priests in the church. It's a matter of focus and distraction. As a married man with four kids, my world is in constant conflict. If I'm at work, I feel like I should be at home chasing kids. On Saturday while mowing the lawn, my mind drifts to market research and PowerPoint presentations. It's a wheel that keeps spinning, and you can never get off the ride. I can't be the only one who feels this way in this day and age.

* * *

My corporate story begins in a typical entry-level sales role in the pharmaceutical industry. Following my brief but memorable theater career, I pursued a master's degree in international business. After graduate school, my new bride and I found ourselves with two master's degrees, no jobs, and living in my old man's basement. We quickly decided that whoever got the first job wins, and that is where we'd settle.

My wife, Heather, won. She took a teaching job at the middle school of my hometown in Washington state, and this left me looking for a corporate entry point in a secondary market. Sales was the fit. It didn't take long to crack open the door of opportunity, and I soon landed a territory job with Hoechst Marion Roussel, the German-US conglomerate which would eventually become today's Sanofi.

My responsibilities included representing allergy and diabetes medications to physicians via office-based sales. I think I started at $37,000. It might as well have been a million dollars. I was in tall cotton. Adding the company car into the mix immediately made me a legitimate contender for the lead headline in my parents' 1999 family Christmas letter. I was a drug rep—the legal kind. We were on our way.

Day One and a Dilemma

The pharmaceutical industry often takes a beating in the press due to the ever-rising price of medicines. Some of the criticism is certainly warranted, but there is an untold side of the story. The business of medicine is tremendously complex, and there is no indication that politicians, in any country, have plans to simplify the process. The rough estimate on the cost to bring a drug from discovery to commercial launch is a billion dollars. Then once the drug is launched, a company only has, at most, twenty years until that drug goes generic. Pile on top that most governments mandate price controls on every product, and the economics of medicine get complicated fast.

Not many business sectors in the world would consider a billion-dollar gamble with a twenty-year commercial window, not to mention the immediate negative press and government market intrusion. But pharma can do it because one in one thousand discoveries is stratospherically successful like Lipitor, Viagra, or Nexium. It's counterintuitive, but we need the occasional overpriced blockbuster drug to keep scientists employed and medical innovation solvent.

Once a drug is on the market, big companies like Pfizer or Johnson & Johnson deploy hundreds of salespeople trained to deliver feature-and-benefit messaging to physicians. It is an effective model requiring professionalism and skill despite the negative press you occasionally hear on cable news. I started my corporate venture with great hope, learned as much as I could about allergy and diabetes, and in no time was out in territory. The exact location of my first sales call is burned into my memory. The weather in Yakima, Washington, was overcast, and I was so nervous I could hardly see straight. It took me an hour to get up the guts to exit my car and enter that office.

Physicians treated me pretty well, and it wasn't too long before I had the basics under control. Then came the bombshell. One day, a news story came out about RU-486, the controversial "morning-after" abortion pill. Although I wasn't too serious in my Catholic endeavors at this point in life, I called myself pro-life, and something in this story caught my attention. Somewhere in the text, seemingly noted as an afterthought, was the name of the company that manufactured this drug: my company. Suddenly, my guaranteed headline in the family Christmas letter seemed fraught with controversy.

I was floored and couldn't believe I worked for that kind of company. Would I have to sell that drug? Internet research was new at the time, so

I pored over any and all related websites. The more I learned about my company's involvement in this issue, the less I understood it. Corporations have a tendency to have business interests in lots of things, but employees may know almost nothing about them because they work in a division completely unattached to the issue. That's what I found in this case.

The US had no plans to market the drug. The World Health Organization, however, was requiring that it be made available. What did that mean? I went from being the star of the Christmas letter in my red Dodge Intrepid to thinking I should quit on ethical grounds. Believe me, the biggest ethical decision I had ever faced at this point was whether or not to take the last beer out of the fridge. I had never even considered I would have to *act* on any serious convictions in my life. Then to add to the joy, it turned out that in the World War II–era the German predecessor company, Hoechst, made the gas that the Nazis used in their sinister campaign of genocide.

Boom. Abortion and nerve gas. Now what?

I just decided to keep my head down and focus on allergy and diabetes. Those medicines were solid and helped patients heal. That would have to be enough. Pretty soon, it was time for our first round of regional meetings, so I thought I would take my findings to my sales team. Certainly, everyone would want to be knowledgeable about this hot issue. I about burned out my dial-up modem as I searched and printed articles until I was satisfied the whole story was uncovered.

On meeting day, we covered the routine issues of sales updates, marketing changes, and new promotional materials. At the end of the session, my boss opened the floor for discussion. I jumped at the chance and brought forth my discovery. The sales team was a bunch of people in their mid-twenties to mid-thirties. That should have been my first clue. I learned a quick lesson about knowing your audience before opening your mouth. My research and concern over the ethical dilemma of working for a company involved in abortion and nerve gas went over like a lead balloon. Silence. Everyone just looked down or out the window. Nobody engaged, agreed, or backed me up. Nobody disagreed. They just sat there with a look I will never forget. The faces in the room were apathetic.

This was the moment I knew I was different. I had a lot to learn for sure, but I was different. My concerns were dismissed, and I was going to have to learn how and when to speak up, as well as when to lay low. My colleagues appeared to not care. Over the years, I have learned that many people actually are concerned about world issues, but speaking up is another matter entirely. In this case, my counterparts around the conference table had heard these issues and appeared to hold no serious opinions on the matter of life. No opinion? Not really, more like they just kept their heads down and didn't speak up.

This was a defining moment. My conscience was as much a part of who I was as my career. Communication from that time forward seemed to operate only at surface level. It wasn't appropriate to have in-depth conversations at work. That was a hard realization to process for a guy who loves to banter.

Fast forward twenty years. Things seem only worse. The world is polarized, divided, and modernistic. If you believe something to be correct, it's correct. Pick your bathroom. Ancient truths are sidelined for individual standards against which nobody can argue, question, or even be curious. This viewpoint spills into the corporate conference room, and people are left trying to solve complex problems within the boundaries of surface-level dialog. Throw Christian conviction into that environment, and you have the makings of a challenging career.

*   *   *

Applied faith in a corporate setting is always tricky. There is a perpetual conflict between the relativism of contemporary culture and the moral concrete of our theology. Conference rooms all over the world become the front lines of the culture wars given that these two world views inevitably collide whenever decisions are to be made. Meetings upon meetings progress daily where folks are looking at the same data, same strategy, and same PowerPoint presentation, but they see the world like apples and oranges.

In order to make sense of our place in this world, the church gives us a moral standard. It is known as the *Catechism of the Catholic Church*. You might call it the "rulebook" at first glance, but it's so much more. The *Catechism* is the compilation of thousands of years of smart writers, from Aquinas to Augustine to Ignatius, who have given great thought and rendered pages of ink on matters of ethics. Prior to the invention of the printing press, matters of church doctrine were primarily passed down via oral tradition. However, early printed versions started popping up in the 1500s, generally following a question-and-answer format.

In perhaps a perfect storm and collision of current events and innovation, the Reformation caught fire in Northern Europe in 1517. The Catholic response to Luther's Ninety-five Theses was the great Council of

Trent. Finished by 1563, the Council of Trent took nearly two decades to complete. The result was a thorough analysis of Luther's complaints and a restating of Catholic truth in a document called the *Roman Catechism* (1566). This completed, comprehensive work on instructing the faithful became a source for all Catholics until its last edition in 1978.[1]

From this first *Catechism* there have been many local and regional works published which aim to properly instruct the faithful. The most famous, and the version your Catholic grandmother would most certainly know, is the *Baltimore Catechism*, first published in 1884. Complete with answers on 421 questions, this is the great work that instructed generations of American Catholics.

Following the Second Vatican Council, where the Mass was changed from Latin to the local language among other things, Pope John XXIII charged church leaders to more effectively "guard the deposit of Christian doctrine" and make it accessible to the people. As such, that brings us up to the present.

Throughout this book, we are referring to the 1992 *Catechism of the Catholic Church*, which was commissioned by Pope John Paul II. This version of the *Catechism* originated from the recommendation of bishops in 1985. Pope (now Saint) John Paul II convened a group to assemble a new, full summary of Catholic teaching, and on December 8, 1992, he submitted the final work. Notably, December 8th is not just the day after Pearl Harbor Day; it is the Feast of the Immaculate Conception. As such, the choice of date was no accident as the pope asked the intercession of the Blessed Virgin Mary, Mother of the Church, to support the evangelization of the faith at every level.[2] The first sentence of John Paul's cover letter that accompanied the submission of the *Catechism of the Catholic Church* tells it all:

> "To my Venerable Brothers the Cardinals, Patriarchs, Archbishops, Bishops, Priests, Deacons, and to all the People of God. Guarding the deposit of faith is the mission which the Lord has entrusted to his Church and which she fulfills in every age."[3]
> —Pope John Paul II, October 11, 1992

---

1. USCCB, *US Catholic Catechism for Adults*, 15–17.
2. *Catechism of the Catholic Church Adult Studies*, "History of the Catechism," https://www.catechism.ie/history-of-the-catechism/.
3. *Catechism of the Catholic Church*, 1.

Day One and a Dilemma

As Catholics, we have the source documents that render the truth. We have the deposit of faith given to us by Christ himself. That right there is enough for me to know there is no need to reinvent the wheel.

Our *Catechism* should be our primary source when considering ethics in the living room, bedroom, or conference room. We are imperfect, and we fall for shenanigans, hucksters, and rock-and-roll pastors with skinny jeans. Thus, we need moral concrete, a platform from which to make decisions. Stay on the lookout for trouble, and keep the truth handy.

* * *

So, what does that mean in the boardroom? How does the *Catechism* come into play in a company setting? It means we have to be compassionate and resolute all at the same time. We know the source from which we draw our decisions and will always be faced with ideas and corporate initiatives that challenge our ethical position.

But the people around us must be approached with compassion and understanding. We cannot simply drop the ethical hammer on people, slam the *Catechism* on their desk, and walk out. That would be a guaranteed trip to HR for a little seminar complete with trust falls, squeeze balls, and in-depth training on hurtful words. We need to communicate major issues with grace and compassion. At the same time, our moral concrete has endured for centuries, without a crack, and that moral concrete *must* inform our decisions at work. The *Catechism* supports us in being resolute in matters of life. Catholic teaching is clear as a bell regardless of our willingness to acknowledge it.

Let's take just one business-related issue that the *Catechism* tackles as a matter of explanation: private ownership. The church position on this issue has been consistent for centuries.

> "The goods of creation are destined for the whole human race. However, the earth is divided up among men to assure the security of their lives, endangered by poverty and threatened by violence. The appropriation of property is legitimate for guaranteeing the freedom and dignity of persons and for helping each of them to meet his basic needs and the needs of those in his charge. It should allow for a natural solidarity to develop between men."[4]

---

4. *Catechism of the Catholic Church*, 2402.

The idea of ownership and stewardship of property draws all the way back to the very beginning of the book of Genesis when man is granted dominion over the earth and its resources. "Be fertile and multiply; fill the earth and subdue it." (Gen 1:28). The word *subdue* is key here, as centuries of scholars and believers have focused on this word actually referring to the territory that each nation must take for itself in order to protect its people and prosper.[5] Thus, the concept of private ownership is established at the very beginning and carries forward consistently in the *Catechism*.

This is just one example of how the documents of our great church can help keep us on the rails, by giving clear reference points as well as unchanging guardrails when considering issues of ethics and morality.

The *Catechism* is the reflection of centuries of thinkers and theologians, many of whom died for the cause, on any issue you can think of: money, wealth, charity, sex, love, war, kids, economics, faith, finance, you name it. We have what we need in order to process complex information and make solid enduring decisions.

---

5. Holy Bible: Catholic Reader's Edition, footnote on Gen 1:28.

4

The Corporate Case for Faith

THE modern corporate world can feel like no place for the faithful. If you don't believe it, try this little test. On Monday morning, grab your coffee mug and head to the break room. Change the subject from the football scores, and run a play-by-play analysis of the Sunday homily. See how long your colleagues stick around when you are not talking about Tom Brady's arm or the Packers' defense.

I've always been intrigued by the phenomenon that is fandom, and I think there is an element of the psychology of the sports fan that can be helpful in standing up for your faith. People love their sports teams. The fans love the history of the Yankee pinstripes and the dozens of championship teams filled with legendary players. Hockey faithful know the Red Wings in and out. Heck, NASCAR people know their favorite driver's brand of tires. Fandom is what connects people to history and tradition within common culture. In Seattle, every other car has a 12th man flag proudly waving in traffic. Evidently, the fans think they are on the squad, too.

Sports fans love to be on the same team. It connects them and binds them to something bigger than themselves. Sounds like religion to me.

Everyone wants to be with a winner. Take the Yankees. They have been winning pennants since 1913. You either love them or you hate them, but even the casual baseball fan has an opinion on the Yankees because they *win*.

Interestingly, the oldest team in baseball is the Cincinnati Reds, who date back to the 1890s. But you won't find as many casual fans who know much about the Reds because they don't have twenty-seven championships like the Bronx Bombers. *Bronx Bombers*. They even have a cool nickname.

It doesn't take a psychologist to agree that people want to be associated with a winner, with the guy who has staying power, with the one who stands out, with the guy with the killer nickname.

Shouldn't that be the case with the Catholic Church? Think about it. Founded in year one by Christ himself, followed by 266 consecutive leaders loaded with personality, scandal, nicknames, victories, and defeats, the Catholic Church is the longest standing team in history. Why aren't we all wearing the jersey of our favorite saint and tailgating before Mass?

The Catholic Church has outlasted empires and monarchies, not to mention sports teams and cultural fads. We go nuts over the Seahawks who have only existed since 1974 but hardly acknowledge the squad with two thousand years of tradition in the trophy case.

Think about the hall of fame. In Cooperstown, the baseball hall of fame has 323 legendary members. The communion of saints has thousands. The first hall-of-fame player formally canonized into sainthood was Saint Ulrich of Augsburg in 993. He was a German bishop known for demanding a high moral standard of himself and others. Since the formal process began, hundreds of saints have earned their trip to canonization by giving their whole life for the team, sometimes enduring martyrdom in violent fashion. The Catholic hall of fame requires far more than batting .334 to be inducted.

I understand that people love to root for their team. But my team is the Catholic Church. It's been around the longest, and Christ himself said it won't be defeated.

Undefeated . . . that's the team whose jersey I want to wear.

*   *   *

Back to Monday morning theology in the break room. The fact of the matter is clear: Corporate America is no place to talk about religion. But I shudder to think where corporate America would be without believers quietly going about the impossible task of living a faith that requires disciplined behavior, love for your fellow man, and adherence to simple, centuries-old, vetted social teachings.

There are plenty of examples where companies have fallen off the ethical rails. We could analyze the implosion of Enron, why Facebook allowed blatant use of private user data, or how cigarette companies get people to pick up a bad habit. The buffet of corporate corruption is long and well stocked with choices. But the bottom line is simple: companies lose their way unless good people stay vigilant and speak up at the critical moments.

As a general rule, companies need people who don't launder money, fudge critical data, overreport earnings, harass the cafeteria lady, or steal sandwiches from the break room. Maybe if the believers can quietly influence at least that much at work, we might get people to think about saving some babies along the way. One thing leads to another, right? On any given day in the office, you'd have better luck talking about international monetary policy with a brownie troop than getting anywhere near the topic of religion.

Others go the opposite route and fall into the culture and go soft on religion altogether. How many retired Catholics do you know? Still others might hang out on Sunday but will simply be a different person on Monday. There's more than one country song about that lifestyle.

So, what are we to do?

Some faithful people quit and drop out of the world altogether. They move to small towns, home school, and create a safe place around their families to the best of their abilities. A guy named Rod Dreher wrote a best seller on this subject. *The Benedict Option*, as it is titled, talks about circling the wagons and creating communities of believers. Live, work, and socialize in community. Start businesses, schools, and colleges with like-minded believers. Bring doctors in who share the faith to hang out a shingle and open a membership-type medical clinic. These are some of the ways the Benedict Option comes to life, and it is happening around the US. This approach simply calls for the rejection of the ridiculous culture that surrounds us and has infiltrated everything. It calls for us to find our people and look out for each other.

I can certainly see the intrigue and attraction of that viewpoint, but I worry about an outflow of believers from major corporations. There must be faithful, God-fearing people of high character in positions of leadership across the corporate world, or we are in for big trouble. Guys like Joseph of Arimathea need to be hunkered down in the trenches, waiting for the moment God needs them for greatness.

What if we take the approach of Thomas Aquinas, "Better to illuminate than merely shine, to deliver to others contemplated truths than merely to contemplate."?

My theory is to be subtly rebellious and quietly exposed as Catholic. Just live it, and let people notice. The world needs godly people, and more of them quickly. So, be the light, and hang in there. You need the paycheck, anyway.

Here are some small rebellious moves to make at work:

1. Keep a small indiscreet crucifix on your desk near your computer monitor. I guarantee someone will ask about it, if they are brave.
2. When someone asks about your weekend, simply start with how great the donuts were after Sunday Mass before you move onto the yardwork update.
3. When talking about the kids, throw in that they read at church, sing in the choir, or help with the fish fry at least half as often as you talk about club volleyball.
4. Always carry a rosary in your pocket. Always. When you are in a meeting and your blood pressure is rising fast, just put a hand in your pocket and pray, "Mother Mary, please help." Our Lady will save you from more than one profanity laced outburst through your career. Guaranteed.

My sense is if I try and stay focused on salvation, I'm in a good spot. It doesn't mean perfection is remotely possible. Perhaps merely sticking it out in the trenches of corporate America is a vocation in itself. Then someday, there just might be a grand cathedral whose namesake is Saint Steve of General Electric, Accounting, Fourth Floor, Third Cubicle on the Right.

* * *

The typical corporate environment is efficiently controlled for appropriate language, monitored for safe subject matter, and contextual communication is the expectation. There has been a lot written about contextual communication, or contextual leadership, and its effectiveness in the business world. The leader on this topic, Rayona Sharpnack, puts it well in her book, *Trade-Up!*.

"Rather than stay mired in the part of their lives that's not working, they trade up to a new mind set or point of view that helps them achieve their dreams and goals."[1]

Sharpnack's point is to speak to colleagues in a way that is effective *and* acceptable. It's all about meeting the person you are talking to where they are and understanding their take on things. If you know where someone is coming from, the better the chance you have to really understand what they are saying. If you know what makes up someone's context and view of life, you more easily know what they mean. This is exactly how you might size someone up for their willingness to accept a conversation on faith. The contextual approach is okay for work and okay for faith. For the most part, it helps people communicate comfortably with each other.

A problem arises when things get uncomfortable by the nature or the gravity of the issue. Then what? What if you simply have to call balls and strikes and get tough? It's possible, but only with a heart centered on an immovable ethical guidepost. When the chips are down and tough decisions are being made, you need to know the context, or worldview, of the folks in that boardroom. And equally important, you need to know your own context and lens by which you see the world. You better know what makes everyone tick before you put them in charge of big stuff. An extreme example might be that you would never put Adolf Hitler in charge of Human Resources. How your people think, their context on the world around them, and their background fuel every single decision in your company.

* * *

Western society mostly identifies as Christian, or believing in God.[2] But we can't really talk about that at work, so one of the main drivers of context and personal morality is off the table in the office. It is critical, then, if you can't ask directly, to know the basics of how a fellow believer might see the world. Let's look at a snapshot of the two primary positions in Christianity: Protestant and Catholic.

Start with John 6 in the New Testament. In case you need a refresher, this is where Jesus institutes the Eucharist by saying about a half-dozen times that unless we eat of his flesh and drink of his blood, we will not have life within us. There is nothing to suggest he is speaking figuratively

1. Sharpnack, *Trade-Up!*.
2. Bolles, *What Color Is Your Parachute?*, 266.

or with some type of symbolism. In the middle of this moment of pure biblical drama, some of the apostles either don't get it or just plain think he's gone mad, and they leave. They walk out. It's the only place in the Gospels where Jesus doesn't redirect his teaching to bring them all back into the moment. If people don't get the Eucharist . . . let them go. Jesus called balls and strikes. Whoa. This is a key moment in history. Some stay and some go, but those that left made that decision on a technicality, and readers are left not knowing if they rejected Christianity entirely. This foreshadows a lot in what would come as the centuries piled up.

In order to understand the staying power of the Catholic Church, it is important to digest and understand the theology and basic historical context of the papacy. Christ launched history's greatest startup in year one, and it must have taken some unbelievable leadership to keep it alive all the way to the present day. Just think of the challenges and incredible odds our church has faced.

In the earliest days of the church, the Roman Empire literally built a spectator sport out of brutally killing Christians. The Colosseum, just across the street from Saint Peter's and the Vatican, was once the place to go and watch gladiators and lions dismember believers. You think English soccer fans are ridiculous? Estimates hold that there are as many as 587 miles of catacombs in Rome.[3] These underground corridors, some four stories deep, are where Christians buried their dead and martyrs for centuries.

To be fair, the Romans weren't completely devoid of humanity. A Christian who was sentenced to death but happened to be a Roman citizen would be *humanely* beheaded. Evidently, having your head chopped off was the concierge service version of the death penalty perhaps with a hot towel, your choice of steamed nuts, and a gin fizz. Regular old noncitizen gentiles convicted of believing in Christ had something less first class in their experience with death. They were brutally crucified and hung on a cross until the buzzards came to pluck out their eyes.

As the centuries racked up, the Roman Catholic Church evolved into what we know it as today. Historical context is important here, although over simplified. As the Roman Empire declined and political chaos took over, the Catholic Church rose into a political power as well as a spiritual leader. By 310, Emperor Constantine had legalized Christianity via the Edict of Milan in a move which pleased his devout mother, Saint Helena.

---

3. Sheen and Morton, *This Is Rome*, 17.

The Corporate Case for Faith

There came a point where the Holy Alliance, which was essentially Catholic-controlled Southern Europe, was under constant threat of attack from the Vikings in the north, Mongols from the East, and the Muslims from the south. Again, oversimplification, but the point is that at no time in church history has there been true tranquility.

Then we can jump a few centuries to the Reformation, when in 1517 Martin Luther shattered the church by posting his Ninety-five Theses on a church door in Wittenberg, Germany. The result was more revolution than reformation. As the Roman Church began to splinter, noble families in Northern Europe claimed churches, real estate, and monasteries for their own. The German Church became Lutheran, and in England, Henry VIII split from the papacy and established himself head of the Church of England.

Violence ensued all over Northern Europe. In England alone, hundreds of convents and monasteries were closed. Catholics were condemned to death, perhaps the most famous being King Henry's right-hand man, Saint Thomas More, who refused to sign the king's required allegiance to his church. Catholics mounted a Counter-Reformation and called to order the Council of Trent, which formally considered all ninety-five of Luther's objections. About half were accepted and reformed, while the other half were rejected on the grounds that the centuries-old theology on those matters was solid. In the end, blood was shed on both sides of the Protestant revolution, and Christendom has never really recovered.

The chaos and aftermath of the Reformation can be seen in any American city. Instead of one holy Catholic Church, it's been estimated there are more than forty thousand Christian denominations as a result. Nobody in their right mind would say that Christians being divided forty thousand different ways was Christ's idea. I've had more than one conversation that goes something like this:

"Would you like to accept Jesus?"

"Already have, thanks."

"Would you come with me to my church?"

"Which one? "

"It's called the Open Door I Love You Church of Jesus and Other Cool Dudes. It's in that strip mall behind the tire shop."

"No thanks, but would you like to come with me to Mass in the cathedral that was built one hundred twenty years ago?"

"No, Catholics aren't Christians."

"Uh, yes, we are, as evidenced by the fact that Christ started the Catholic Church and that very same church has protected and handed down Christ's teachings for centuries."

"But you worship Mary."

"Not quite. Would you like me to explain the theology of Mary to you?"

"No. Bye."

Christianity is divided along lines of misunderstanding and self-analysis of theology, which is a travesty. As noted earlier, this exemplifies personal context entering into everything. Imagine if humanity could actually get it together and operate from one moral worldview, the one established by Christ himself. Put another way, what if it was actually good versus evil? In the current world, evil is fully united, yet there are forty thousand versions of good. The cultural phenomenon of "you be you" or "live your best life" seems to have left us all defining morality for ourselves. This is obvious trouble, given the reality that confusion tends to set in when a group of people are not 100 percent aligned. How much better would companies run, governments function, and communities live together if we were actually united in the definition of goodness?

Luther of all people said it best as he neared his death:

> "I must confess that my doctrines have produced many scandals. I cannot deny it, and often this frightens me, especially when my conscience reminds me that I destroyed the situation in which the Church found itself, all calm and tranquil, under the Papacy."[4]

The answer is extremely complex, and this book is not a treatise on the Reformation. But as we consider our faith in this modern world, where everything seems to be acceptable, it is important to know where that worldview sprouted from.

The Reformation left Christendom fractured with two primary themes that came to be known as *sola Scriptura* and *sola fide*. The first, *sola Scriptura*, is the premise that the individual should be their own interpreter of Scripture. You read the Bible and come up with your own idea of what it means. And the Bible is the sole authority or source of teaching. Sounds good on the surface, but imagine if we took that approach with physics and engineering. Think for a moment the result if they took that approach with the Golden Gate Bridge. "Hey, you, here's the drawings. Figure them out

---

4. Moczar, *Ten Dates Every Catholic Should Know*, 99.

The Corporate Case for Faith

for yourself, run whatever calculations you see fit, and get to work." Who is ever going to drive over that contraption?

It is a ridiculous notion to disregard the great thinkers that came before us in a subject as critical as engineering. The same holds true for faith. Aquinas, Augustine, Saint Thérèse of Lisieux, Tertullian, and all the others gave us divine insight into the scriptures. All told, about one hundred famous writers and theologians have earned the title Doctor of the Church. These writers, most who lived prior to the seventh century, are where the great tradition of the Catholic Church resides.[5] They are the teachers who read the same books we do, lived under the same moral code we do, and wrote about it. Their writings are a gift that upholds Christ's message rather than redefines it. There is no reason to go it alone.

The second main theme of the Reformation is *sola fide*, or faith alone. This premise is that once you accept Christ as savior, you are clear. Heaven awaits, and there is nothing left on your spiritual to-do list. As Catholics, we bring it back to the Bible where we are clearly called to put faith in action. We are called to work for the betterment of the world.

> "Indeed someone may say, 'You have faith and I have works.' Demonstrate your faith to me without works, and I will demonstrate my faith to you from my works."
>
> —James 2:18

Christ set his disciples in motion to work for the kingdom. Just look at the book of Acts, where the apostles, after the ascension of Christ, set out around the Mediterranean to preach the gospel, set up churches, appoint priests and deacons, and in many cases, die for the great commission. Even more crystal clear, there is no reason whatsoever for a book in the Bible called Acts if we are not called to *do something* about our faith.

In the end, the Reformation was more about rejecting papal authority than it was rejecting doctrine. Most Christian denominations are fairly aligned in the big picture of Jesus and his teaching. That's the good news. The trouble is that with the world beginning to call their own shots as far back as 1517, we end up in a position whereby the individual is interpreting their own definition of right and wrong. Then things go off the rails.

Okay, how does this all fit into the conference room on a typical day at work?

---

5. Aquilina, *The Fathers of the Church*.

Again, back to the original premise: Christ started this whole thing with nothing. No money, no station in life, and no organization behind him. And after about three years of work, he was brutally killed. The project barely got off the ground before he was eliminated, sold out by the Jews and killed by the Romans. Since then, millions of his followers have also been martyred. How did this thing survive twenty minutes after the crucifixion, much less two thousand years? Martin Luther was upset with corruption and human failing in the church, and honestly, he was right in issuing his list of grievances. But anyone who has ever attempted to cause change or negotiate the terms of a deal knows that if you get 50 percent of what you originally ask for, you are doing pretty well. Reform is what Luther wanted, but revolution is what he caused.

The Catholic response to the Reformation came at the Council of Trent, which agreed on reform of half of Martin Luther's complaints. If the church responded, it is a legitimate question to ask why the Reformers continued to break apart the church? Christ left us something concrete to believe. He gave us moral teachings and established leadership and a beautiful way to worship. All these things work together to give the faithful a leg up on the chaos that surrounds us in the world.

A Catholic in a corporate setting should know exactly what the church believes. He should know his moral position on any corporate decision because of our Catholic history. If we have questions, all we have to do is grab a *Catechism*, and the answers are there for the taking. The *Catholic Catechism* offers two thousand years of analysis on politics, war, love, sex, finance, economics, international relations, children, government, wages, and the list goes on. The issues have been tackled. The rulebook is clear. We are not left with *sola Scriptura* and the overwhelming responsibility of starting from scratch in order to analyze and determine our take on the world. There is no guesswork to be done in matters of being a good steward of your business and community.

In the end, both the public and private sectors are far better off if caring, diligent Catholics are working, leading, and guiding organizations. God needs us in the trenches. Remember that the next time you are ten cups of coffee into a long day, calling balls and strikes in the boardroom.

5

Ash Wednesday at the Sales Meeting

It ain't easy being faithful. It really ain't easy at a company meeting. The booze normally flows, the nights are late, and the jokes get filthier as the week progresses. Fatigue sets in by about Wednesday, and the easiest path can be to just surrender and drink your way to the flight home. There's no taking a night off. A company man participates, showing no signs of wearing out. That's the bottom line. I've stood at the taxi stand at the MGM Grand and poured more than one hungover VP into a cab.

A national conference can be tough for the majority who straddle the fence of discipline with keeping up with the executives. Holy days add another element to the mix when you're out of town at a meeting. What a joy the beginning of Lent can be in that scenario.

Working for a big pharma company certainly has its lodging benefits. No need to leave a light on for us down at Motel 6. Most corporations spare little expense to retain talented folks. A decent hotel, good food, and free drinks go a long way to keeping people engaged while away from home.

Meetings all run together. If you've been to enough of them, the speakers sound the same, and the buzzwords are recycled session over session. Occasionally, it gets interesting when someone gets too drunk at the bar, speaks their incoherent mind on an issue, and ends up reprimanded (or promoted).

For the most part, people just want to get in, grab the binders with the relevant information, and get home. Five minutes after any given meeting concludes, nobody remembers much content. It doesn't matter if you are manufacturing shoes, pharmaceuticals, or bobblehead dolls. The meetings are the same. There is one meeting, however, that I remember vividly. It was in Dallas, and we arrived on Fat Tuesday.

Me and the only other identifiable Catholic guy got up early Wednesday morning. We had heard there was a church in the vicinity and looked up the Mass time for Ash Wednesday. 6:00 a.m. Fair enough. At a company meeting, you have to be up early to wrestle a full helping of powdered eggs and cold bacon anyway. An early bell is no big deal. If you are trying to get promoted, a 5:00 a.m. stroll through the hotel gym is also advised.

We jumped in a cab that the bellhop flagged for us. As we told the guy where to take us, he immediately became irate. Clearly of international descent, and potentially a fan of Mecca, we just concluded the source of his anger was that he didn't want to drive two dirty Romans to Mass. Come to find out, a block later, that the church was directly behind the hotel. It couldn't have been any closer. Literally, the church was probably fifty paces from the back lobby door.

This poor guy probably slept in his taxi, waiting for a lucrative airport run. Then two idiots show up for a one-block ride and a total fare of about thirty-five cents. As he screamed at us in his best Arabic slang, I threw him a twenty, and we were safely out of the minivan. I'm not even sure he came to a full stop.

* * *

Any good Catholic knows that Ash Wednesday is a great moment. It is the ancient, reverent center point marking the beginning of Lent. Believers go out of the way once a year to gather and mark the beginning of a forty-five-day period of abstinence, fasting, and almsgiving. That day always seems to fall somewhere in the annual corporate meeting calendar cycle. It doesn't matter where a Catholic may be on Ash Wednesday. You have to drop everything and get to church.

Ash Wednesday at the Sales Meeting

On a quick sidenote, we Catholics are a gathering people. We make it a point to worship together. Paul sums up that notion in his letter to the Hebrews as he reminds the faithful "We should not stay away from our assembly, as is the custom of some, but encourage one another." (Heb 10:25). To that end, it's always nice to have a corporate wingman on Catholic holy days.

I've tried to give up booze for Lent, but that's tough in a company meeting setting. Of course, Jesus had it 20,000 percent tougher. I know. I'm just weak. I can't be the only one.

The tradition of taking ashes on the forehead is the quintessentially Catholic tradition, and it can be a beautiful thing to see celebrities and pundits on TV showing, by the ashes, their commitment to the faith on Ash Wednesday. For the company man, it can be a tough day. Most of us aren't on TV. We have to go back to work where most people don't get the whole routine. Thus, Ash Wednesday inevitably comes with spending all day with people saying, "Hey, Meyer, there's dirt on your face."

There is always a priest who seemingly has a bone to pick with your forehead. The strategy is to let the situation unfold and watch how the congregation is coming back with their ashes. It's always a mix of artistry. One guy will have a cross stretching ear to ear and crown to nose. Another will have just a tiny cross that looks more like a dot. That's the line you want to get in. Otherwise, you're facing a long day of strange looks from the great corporate unchurched.

Ash Wednesday, if taken at surface level, doesn't look like much more than marking the beginning of Lent with ashes. But going deeper into the symbolism and process of ritual is what makes it come alive.

Catholics are no strangers to ritual, and in my opinion, that is a big element of what makes our religion great. Will Durant said it best in his book *The Story of Civilization*:

> "In every great religion, ritual is as necessary as creed. It instructs, nourishes, and often begets belief; it brings the believer into comforting contact with his God; it charms the senses and soul with drama; poetry and art; it binds individuals into a fellowship and a community by persuading them to share in the same rites, the same prayers, at last the same thoughts."[1]

---

1. Durant, *The Story of Civilization*.

The greatest display of all Catholic ritual is the Mass itself. From the moment the priest enters the sanctuary, every single element of the liturgy is dragging along with it a couple thousand years of tradition.

Anyway, back to the story. I lost the ash strategy and ended up with a cross that spanned ear to ear and hairline to nose brim. It was 7:00 a.m., and I was facing a big day of stare-downs and "dirty face" comments. I could hear it as I walked back to the hotel for a few minutes before the day's sessions began: "Hey, Meyer. Is there buried treasure under that receding hairline?"

Once in my room, I stared at the mirror and couldn't bring myself to face an entire day standing out like a Republican at a vegan conference. I guess in that moment, I experienced a crisis of faith. The conversation with me and myself went something like this:

"I believe. I went to Mass. Isn't that enough?"

"Depends," said the man in the mirror.

"Depends on what!" I fired back, suddenly realizing I was living a Michael Jackson song.

"On whether or not your depth of faith matters."

Whoa.

"On whether your depth matters."

Checkmate for the mirror.

The Almighty doesn't wait long to tell us how he expects us to show up in life. The very first book of the Bible gives us a clue. Adam and Eve, by the covenant with God, are given the gift of paradise. But it comes with the cost of obedience. Obedience is our first required act of faith. The symbolism and traditions of the Catholic faith help us test our metal and hopefully strengthen our obedience to God. Ash Wednesday is one of those great traditions that firmly place our faith on the outside of ourselves and display it to everyone else. One day a year, we all have to wear the Catholic billboard.

In a moment of weakness, I compromised. I washed off the outer edges of my ashes and left a small cross in the middle of my forehead. I went down to the meeting and, session by session, soaked up topics and business details I can't recall. I was fully engaged in the corporate charge but simultaneously compromising my faith. Predictably, I spent the day answering the "dirty face" questions I had set out to avoid.

Plus, I also spent the day answering this question from the other guy who joined me for the one-block taxi ride to Mass: "Wasn't that cross on your face a lot bigger coming out of Mass?"

6

The Orthodox Cabbie

THE best education takes place in taxicabs. If you engage a taxi driver in conversation, you will be granted wisdom. If you press it and cause an argument, you might get taken the long way to your hotel, but if you can handle the extra fare, you'll end up with a PhD in life. I've been yelled at, ripped off, given history lessons, lectured, and dealt with many an unusual stench. But the life-changing lesson I received in California early one morning was awesome.

I was at a meeting in an Orange County hotel. The purpose of the meeting I can no longer recall, but for some reason, I needed to run to the airport at sunrise and pick up a rental car. The morning was typically California beautiful. Crisp air and an ocean breeze greeted me as I walked out the door of the hotel to the bell stand. There's a reason why people put up with California's ridiculous politics and craziness. Nothing beats the beauty of a warm, crisp, coastal morning. It must be the gift provided by the Holy Spirit for putting up with all the traffic.

A yellow minivan pulled up, and I jumped in wearing my flip-flops, coffee in hand. I had meetings at nine, so I was getting this rental car business out of the way early. For the first few minutes, I didn't say anything and just enjoyed the scenery.

Then I noticed a cross hanging from the rearview mirror. Without thinking, I blurted out something like, "Hey, I like your cross." The driver, who I really hadn't sized up at this point, looked at me through the mirror, and we made eye contact. He was huge. Like three bills huge. He continued staring at me, not looking at the road, for what seemed like forever. Finally, he spoke.

"Yes. I am believer," he said. His accent was deep and his English broken. Mediterranean, maybe? I didn't know yet. His voice was deeper. "I am Greek. Greek Orthodox. You?"

Uh . . . "Catholic."

He then finally looked back at the road in silence, almost like he was deciding how much of a lesson I could absorb at six in the morning.

"You and me. We are brothers. What happened in fourth century was wrong. We are brothers."

Right there, I was already lost. "Fourth century?"

My massive taxi-driving professor then launched into a ten-minute history lesson on the schism of the Eastern Church. I was in awe of his passion and his knowledge. Of course, he could tell me anything, as I was clueless. He sounded smart, was very passionate about it, and was in control of my destiny. So, I bought it.

In the years since this experience, I have been increasingly curious about the history of the church and how we ended up here. It's worth the investment of a few paragraphs to try and set up where my cabbie buddy was coming from that morning. There are actually multiple churches, twenty-four to be exact, that are in alignment with Rome. They align theologically and recognize the pope, but they do not submit to papal authority. The vast majority of us—over ninety percent of Catholics—align to the Latin rite so are tied directly to Rome. The rest are Eastern rite churches, as they have come to be called.

The Roman Church dates back to Peter himself, whereby his mission of evangelization led him to the heart of the empire. Peter continued to evangelize in Rome until his crucifixion in the year 64. Evidently, he wanted to be crucified upside down, as he felt unworthy to go out the same way as Christ. Tradition has held that Peter's tomb on Vatican Hill is located under Saint Peter's Basilica. The largest church building in the world was originally built over the Circus of Nero by Emperor Constantine. It was later rebuilt in the 1500s, using stone from the Roman Colosseum. Peter's tomb has since been located and excavated under the basilica. Its discovery was announced to the world in 1950. "The tomb of the Prince of the Apostles has been found," Pope Pius XII proclaimed via radio.

There is no way to know with absolute certainly that the remains found are Peter's. However, significant archeological evidence makes for a very strong case, in particular an inscription that was found in the wall that says *Petros Eni* . . . or "Peter is here." Nonetheless, there is no doubting Peter's historical impact on Rome in terms of building what would become the Catholic Church. From the earliest centuries, the church in Rome was able to get up on its feet, and even under intense persecution, continued to grow.

Following the great commission where Jesus extolled the apostles to proclaim the news to the ends of the earth, they fanned out to all corners of the Roman Empire. They started churches, appointed bishops, and established liturgy in communities and outposts all over the Mediterranean. We can see this history unfold through each of the letters of the New Testament. All told, the apostles wrote twenty-one letters to the faithful, which ended up in the Bible. Many others were written and are considered great works if not included in the biblical canon. Each letter formed liturgy, fought against heresy, and encouraged the new leaders of the early church. Letter after letter showcases a group of fledgling church leaders trying to guide the faith with consistency, structure, and accountability.

It is no surprise that the early church had trouble getting off the ground and keeping everything on the rails. The forces working against the first missionaries were nearly insurmountable, and most ended up martyred. Yet here we are two thousand years later with millions of Christians living under daily persecution *today*, and Christ's church survives. In my opinion, that must be the Holy Spirit at work, and we cannot ignore it.

* * *

The first Roman emperor to embrace the faith was Constantine, who, by issuing his Edict of Milan in 313, finally legalized Christianity. Constantine's proclamation didn't mean that it was all peaches and cream for Christians from that point, but it was the beginning of bringing the faith out from the underground.

It is important to note that the Roman Empire eventually grew to a point that it had to be governed by an Eastern and Western emperor, and Constantine was the first to align with this new Christian worldview. As the centuries wore on, the Western half of the empire was the first to fall in 476, but by this point, the Roman Catholic Church was for all intents and purposes established. The papacy was located in Rome, and although the Christian population was persecuted, it remained strong.

The Eastern Empire was a different story. Centuries of Roman corruption collided with ever-rising Muslim dominance. Ever shifting and conflicting power made it difficult for the Christian church to maintain theological control, much less alignment and consistency with Rome.

There were arguments and division between Roman rite popes and Eastern rite patriarchs. The first problem arose when Emperor Constantius appointed an Arian heretic as patriarch. Pope Julian excommunicated the patriarch in 343, and Constantinople remained in schism until John Chrysostom assumed the patriarchate in 398. This type of back and forth between Rome and Constantinople continued and has unfortunately persisted to this day. The final blow really came when the Byzantine Empire, another name for the remaining eastern Roman Empire, collapsed in 1453. Under pressure from Muslims, Christian patriarchs were often instilled for purposes of power, or bought and paid for influence. From 1453 to 1923, Turkish sultans deposed 105 out of 159 patriarchs.[1]

The good news is that all twenty-plus Catholic churches are nearly identical in doctrine, and the Vatican considers each in full communion with Rome. Nobody can say the Catholic Church is not diverse and inclusive. There is also the hope that the Eastern and Roman Churches will fully reconcile in the not-too-distant future.

* * *

Back to the story of my new friend in the cab. As the sun came up and the highway began to fill with cars, I sat in awe of my new brother. He knew his stuff, and he believed it. He believed that we were better together as brothers in Christ. You could feel it in that car. It was divine. Better together. That's one of our corporate slogans. Imagine it, corporate slogans being biblical. Then he really floored me as we came down an off-ramp to a stoplight.

---

1. Catholic Answers, "Eastern Orthodoxy," https://www.catholic.com/tract/eastern-orthodoxy.

"This cab," he started, and again, he was looking at me in the mirror and not at the road. I guessed we were safe since it was a red light. He continued, unaffected by the traffic signals. "This is my church. I have to work always to feed my family. I cannot go to church. This car, this is my church."

He continued staring into my soul via the rearview as he gestured the sign of the cross. "So, in my car I say my prayers."

I sat frozen by the moment.

"I work, eat, pray in this car. But I am embarrassed."

"What?" I finally said with an embarrassed tone. The voice in my head was wondering how someone that huge, with that much presence, could ever be embarrassed.

"I pray, but I pull up short. Like this light. I have to pray, but I don't want guy next to me to see. So, I stop behind window of his car. He not see me pray. Embarrassing that I cannot let faith be seen."

"I don't understand," I said, which was true of the whole conversation at this point.

"I tell you, I am embarrassed to pray. I got so mad at myself. You know what I do now?"

Now I was getting nervous. The light was still red. He wasn't looking anywhere at the road or intersection, and he was getting more and more passionate.

"I say no more," he said, voice rising as he hammered the dashboard with his fist. "No more pull up short. No more hide. Now I pull up, right up to the window of other car. I pull up. Roll down window. Look at other driver. Then I smile. Make sign of cross . . . and I say my prayers."

"No more hiding," he said as his voice trailed off, and he appeared to realize he needed to pay attention to the road.

Holy crap. No more hiding. That might be the single greatest challenge to living the faith ever issued. Believe it because it's true, and don't hide. So simple yet convicting. I have no idea what this guy's name was, but I'm sure the Almighty sent him to get my attention. These people who keep showing up in some interesting or mysterious way is a theme across my career. He called me out dead to rights. I'm the master chameleon when it comes to reading a room and changing my colors. How many of us can talk trash or talk sports. I can talk shallow or go deep. If your title is bigger, my opinions are yours. Late in the bar, I can rack up the frat brother lingo and dominate the filthy jokes. Blend in, it's easier.

We went on about our conversation for a few more minutes. I parted from my new brother shortly thereafter at the John Wayne Airport, but I would now have to view myself from a new lens. Prior to this moment, I would have never categorized myself as the guy who hid from anything. I was in it to win it and fully engaged. Just read my performance reviews. They clearly stated that I am outstanding. Yet the giant Greek was broadcasting a message for every corporate chameleon.

I recall the story of the apostles hiding in the upper room. Following their cowardly betrayal of Jesus, they were scared, had no options, and were all wanted men. The Romans and the Jews were bound and determined to wipe out whoever remained of Christ's ragtag band of followers. Peter even thought about going back to fishing. But at some point, they all came to the same conclusion as my giant cabbie. At some point, somebody stood up and said, "Enough! Let's get on with it, and change the world."

* * *

I keep running into these kinds of guys. Over the last twenty years of corporate travel, I have probably racked up over six hundred thousand miles on one airline, not to mention a couple hundred thousand miles on airlines that only fly to Sheboygan. I've been in high-end hotels in most major cities. I have had more steaks at Morton's and Ruth's Chris than my colon should have ever been tasked to process. Been there and ordered the molten chocolate cake.

For some reason, however, there are always these little moments where something spectacular evolves. That moment in Australia was the first one, then the LA cabbie, and a few more you have yet to read about. As a result of these moments where I clearly feel I'm being asked to do more, I have resolved over the years to force myself at least to mention my faith. Thus, perhaps I get myself into these situations with my own mouth. Who knows? But I can tell you in no uncertain terms that the Holy Spirit is gunning for me and for you. All you have to do is mention that you are Catholic once in a while, and powerful things happen. Try it.

As for this situation, the giant Greek cabbie's conviction was the challenge. He took me apart and put me back together better than any corporate 360-degree feedback session. His point was simple: no more hiding. We are called to get to a point where we are confident in our faith and are willing to claim it. We cannot live within two contradicting worldviews. We cannot be faithful and secular at the same time, or we will all fall into unresolvable conflict with ourselves.

The biggest example I can think of is abortion. What is your position? It's either a tiny human being with its own unique and distinct DNA and must be protected with all the rights the rest of us enjoy, or it's not and can be discarded. There's no middle ground.

Once we decide a baby can be eliminated, we risk discarding other people as valueless. Abortion on demand for minors without parental consent comes to mind. Euthanasia of the elderly as an affordable medical option is a frightening reality that is already legal in multiple states. Or, transgender counseling that effectively channels a confused young person to permanent surgical sexual reassignment with little or no parental input. People talk about the slippery slope, and it all comes from the simple fact that too many of us try to live on the fence. Whether we have realized it or not, there is no middle ground. Riding the fence ultimately creates more suffering than if we would just hold to the moral teachings in the first place. Our document from the Pontifical Council for Justice and Peace continues to provide great insight into the church's teaching:

> "Compartmentalizing the demands of one's faith from one's work in business is a fundamental error that contributes to much of the damage done by businesses in our world today, including overwork to the detriment of family or spiritual life, an unhealthy attachment to power to the detriment of one's own good, and the abuse of economic power in order to make even greater economic gains."[2]

Thus, my cabdriver brother knew from experience and was trying to tell me in no uncertain terms that living a double life is impossible.

Christ either died to save our souls and bring us the kingdom of heaven, or it's just a story that oddly won't go away. It's all or nothing. If the story of Christ is real, we should be floored and frozen in awe by his majesty at Sunday Mass, and all decisions between Sundays must be driven and informed by the *Catechism*. If it's all just a first-century joke, then we're clear to cash it in and grab the remote, forget Mass, and watch the Dolphins game. The point I think my giant cabbie evangelist made is simple. We are called to be all in. In order to do so, we must think, pray, analyze, and conclude once and for all that our faith is everything.

---

2. Pontifical Council for Justice and Peace, "Vocation of the Business Leader," 5.

Then we are to take it to work. Remember those small rebellious moves I mentioned in chapter 4? Here's a shorter version:

1. Keep an indiscreet crucifix on your desk.
2. Mention Mass in your conversations.
3. Talk about your kids' involvement at church.
4. Always carry a rosary in your pocket.

By doing these little things at work you might even change the world, just like that cabbie changed mine.

No more hiding.

7

268 Slides

THERE is a classic urban legend of the business world about market research. In the early eighties, Chevrolet introduced the new model Nova. I'm sure about half of the families in my little town had a Chevy Nova. It was the Honda Pilot of its time. They were all over the roads.

When it came time to begin selling the Nova in markets outside the US, Chevy introduced the car in Mexico. To say the least, it was a failure. The new model family sedan with all the bells and whistles did not sell. It was a failure from the very start. Evidently, it was a major head-scratcher in corporate meetings in Detroit. The big boys wanted answers to the Mexican sales dilemma. Turns out it was all in the name.

Nova in Spanish sounds like no va, which translates to "doesn't go." Oops. Chevy's market research overlooked a simple yet critical element that ultimately killed the international hopes for the brand.

"Can we interest you in a Nova? It really isn't worth a crap."

If you are a company man working on a brand, market research is a necessary discipline. Research is intricate and exact. Every major corporation spends millions on market research. It can be the difference between a billion-dollar success and a brand that no va.

The problem with market research is that the process will put the average man into a deep sleep quicker than a viewing of The Notebook. Most market research comes together over months of developing testing protocols, fine-tuning preliminary messaging, and recruiting participants. Then there is the process itself where market researchers try out their hypotheses via in-person questioning of target consumers who agree to the process of being monitored by the research team that sits behind the smoky glass. It's kind of like what you see in police movies when they interrogate the perp. In the end, the final product is a PowerPoint deck with up to five hundred slides which illustrate the reactions and recommendations of thousands of points of input. That's just the collection part of the process.

Once you have the data, the task of boiling down and explaining it to your company kicks off. People fly in from all over the country and settle into long, long meetings where every one of the five hundred research slides are considered. These meetings are legendary for an immense amount of charts, data, slides, and the minutiae that needs to be discussed. The funny part is watching the sales guys endure these nine-hour long-haul meetings.

Astronauts and engineers are wired for detail and precision. Market researchers are a similar breed. Sales guys—well, the good ones, anyway—are wired to hustle and move. Asking these guys to attend a three-day research read-out is like asking a two-year-old to stand at attention in a bouncy house. Impossible.

I sat in a three-day, all-day research and planning extravaganza recently. By end count, we reviewed 268 PowerPoint slides. From the first fancy data set to the last, the research and operations teams were riveted by the information. The salesmen were ready to leap out the window after twenty minutes.

People-watching is the fun part of these meetings. Some people can handle detail but not ambiguity. Some people can handle chaos but not detail. Humanity is wonderfully diverse, different, and strange. That is what makes us interesting and bearable to our fellow man. As I sat in that research meeting, I couldn't help ponder the intersection of religion in all of it.

* * *

Jesus knew all too well that people are created individually to be very, very unique. Some people see the world in detail, just as others see the world in the abstract. Right handers and left handers, all eight billion of us see the world from a little different lens. Our savior knew exactly how to communicate a message, which would resonate for centuries, with zero market research. He had no access to an expensive consulting agency and no PowerPoint.

In Mark's Gospel, Jesus talks of the simplicity of the faith. Love God. Love your Neighbor. "Take courage, it is I, do not be afraid!" (Mark 6:50). Somehow, this message is capable of sinking deep into the soul of every kind of human personality. No test questions or smoky glass necessary.

The Baltimore *Catechism* sets up what Christ knew all too well: "No human being can live properly unless he knows the purpose of life."[1] If knowing our purpose allows us to live properly, then that sense of purpose will also grant freedom and peace of mind at the end of the road. Jesus knew that as people seek purpose, they ask questions until they run right into God. I don't think there is any other end to that road. Look continuously for purpose and truth. Find God. End of story. Simple.

There are countless philosophers and great thinkers who found their way to the Catholic Church by seeking purpose over time. Saint John Henry Newman (1801–1890) is a good example of a great intellect who God took all the way to Rome. Newman was a well-known intellectual, poet, and writer. He was an academic at Oxford and priest in the Anglican Church. As the story goes, Newman found great interest in the deep tradition and rituals rooted in Catholicism, and he participated in a movement to return those rituals to the English Church. Ultimately, he became a Catholic priest and cardinal. Newman could not deny that truth resides and springs forth from the Catholic Church. He was canonized a saint in 2019.

As much as thinkers and intellectuals are drawn to the church through study and research, the opposite seems to also happen with many of us. "Too many rules," people will say. To be sure, the *Catechism* sitting here on my desk has 2865 labeled sections, and at first glance, it looks a bit

---

1. Baltimore *Catechism* No. 3, 6.

like the US tax code. Who would ever play Monopoly if you had to read a thousand-page book of rules before you bought Park Place?

The concepts of "rulebook" and "moral platform" are interchanged and misplaced in our modern language. The two terms mean different things entirely. The idea of morality stirs in most of us the notion of a big, long list of what people cannot do with their life.

"Can you believe this! It says right here I can't have thirty girlfriends, rob a bank, or pound fifteen beers a day. Who do these people think they are?"

If we actually differentiate between morality and rules, we can find that morality grants true freedom, while rules, more simplistically, demand only compliance.

Modern society loves rules but tends to reject morality. To board an airplane, we happily comply with an ever-growing list of articles of clothing we need to remove. We almost worship the NFL, and everyone just accepts without question the three hundred plus rules that govern each game. To buy a house, you have to fill out 137 pages of paperwork and give the bank everything but a stool sample. There are rules surrounding and piling up around us all the time, and we don't even notice. But mention morality, and it's grounds for a food fight at the Thanksgiving table. Think about it this way: if society was truly, truly focused on morality, then abortion could be completely legal, and yet not a single unborn baby would ever be harmed. We need the rules.

The Catholic Church has stated the case for morality without shifting, drifting, or following trends for two thousand years. To me, that little fact is liberating. The church has never resorted to researching social trends to determine direction which tells me, in this world of almost overwhelming "anything goes" type input from the media and entertainment, we can trust that we have a clear source for truth in our ancient documents. The *Catechism* goes to great lengths to break down and explain the moral platforms of the church and then illustrate that the path to the good life begins with a pretty simple approach. This notion is brought into the light in the first paragraph of the prologue of our *Catechism*:

> "God, infinitely perfect and blessed in himself, in a plan of sheer goodness freely created man to make him share in his own blessed life. For this reason, at every time and in every place, God draws close to man. He calls man to seek him, to know him, love him with all his strength. He calls together all men, scattered and divided by sin, into the unity of his family, the Church. To accomplish this, when the fullness of time had come, God sent his Son as

Redeemer and Savior. In his Son and through him, he invites men to become, in the Holy Spirit, his adopted children and thus heirs of his blessed life."[2]

God set the whole thing up so that we can achieve perfection. Okay, I'm listening. Perhaps our "Catholic rules" have a little deeper purpose than simply operating as a punitive list of *don'ts*. Perhaps they are there in order to keep us on the rails throughout life. And being on the rails is actually the most guaranteed ticket to perfect happiness.

Secular culture tells us that God is like a 437-slide PowerPoint presentation. He demands that we pay attention to way too many unnecessary details. Faith is just too complicated and rigid. But Christ and his church are really asking the opposite of each and every one of us. Christ is asking us to keep it simple. Life is better lived within the guardrails of love and morality than on the trampoline of "anything goes."

The answers are there for the finding if we listen to our faith. If you want to boil it down to a minimum, the church sets out five moral precepts (CCC 2042):

1. You shall attend Mass on Sundays and holy days of obligation.
2. You shall confess your sins once a year.
3. You shall receive the sacrament of the Eucharist at least during the Easter season.
4. You shall observe the days of fasting and abstinence.
5. You shall help provide for the needs of the church.

The Catechism explains how life will evolve if these five basic rules are followed: "The obligatory character of these positive laws decreed by the pastoral authorities is meant to guarantee to the faithful the very necessary minimum in the spirit of prayer and moral effort, in the growth in love of God and neighbor." (CCC 2041).

Let's break that statement down like a market researcher:

1. The laws are positive, not negative or punitive.
2. They represent the minimum effort needed to cause a result.
3. The result will be greater love of God and neighbor.

---

2. *Catechism of the Catholic Church*, "Prologue."

Christ didn't need marketing or research or complex messaging. He told us clearly how to live our best life. If we all start here and at least get to Mass on Sundays and confession once in a while, we can then use the rest of the *Catechism* to help guide life's big decisions.

Our faith has compiled centuries of teachings, writings, and analysis on the matter. 266 popes have weighed in on theological issues as well as thousands of great thinkers and martyrs. In corporate settings, we think nothing of sitting through hours and hours of research findings, compliance training, regulatory briefings, or product updates. Details and rules are everywhere, and nobody blinks an eye. As believers and the leaders of faith in our families, men need to start standing up for the need for detailed moral structure which can guide us straight to the good life.

Jesus always taught in simple, straightforward terms: "Whoever believes and is baptized will be saved; whoever does not believe will be condemned." (Mark 16:16).

We readily accept rules in every aspect of life. Why do we think we are off the hook regarding the rules when related to morality?

8

Waffle House

Pull off the highway, and grab a table at Waffle House. Then sit back and open your ears. You might just meet Thomas Aquinas, Aristotle, or even Saint Peter himself. Order an All-Star Breakfast at 2:00 a.m., put the phone down, and hold on for the ride. These roadside joints are loaded with characters who might just change your viewpoint on the world.

This Waffle House story transpired late one night somewhere in Alabama. Our flight arrived at 11:00 p.m. in Atlanta, and we were on the road to Tuscaloosa. My daughter and I were on a college visit in Alabama to check out the Crimson Tide. Rosie, our second daughter, was bound and determined to find a college that met two criteria: It was big and somewhere warm—and it could be afforded by Mom and Dad.

In our family, the college-visit trips fall on me, while the move-ins and dorm decorating fall on my wife. Our first daughter ended up at Hillsdale College in Michigan, and it was partly due to my corporate travel habits.

She wanted to visit Miami of Ohio. She had read somewhere that they had a good journalism school. So, we put together a trip to visit a couple schools in the Ohio Valley area. Anyway, long story short, we flew to Detroit because I fly Alaska Airlines, and that's as close as we could get on free tickets. That dictated the stopover at Hillsdale. Her mother wanted her to look at Hillsdale, but she wasn't buying it.

"Great idea, Mom," said no kid ever.

It all changed when we drove up the hill toward campus. I had my speech all cued up to layout the reason why we had to go on the tour and not just decide it was no good from a drive-by. She was sold the moment we pulled into the parking lot.

You can't predict what your kids choose any better than you can predict what experience you're going to stumble into at over an All-Star at 2:00 a.m.

* * *

With one off to college at Hillsdale, it was time to find a school for kid number two, and as previously mentioned, we were in search of someplace warm. Of course, I could buy a lot of sweaters and space heaters for the $60,000 Alabama wanted in tuition. But we had to start somewhere. It was 1:00 a.m., and we were passing through Moody, Alabama, on the way to Tuscaloosa.

"Dad, I'm hungry," said the teenager.

"Let's hit the Waffle House," I suggested.

At this moment, I'd never set foot in a Waffle House before, so I had no expectations. We pulled off the highway, and there were two locations, one on either side. This must have been some brilliant marketer's idea on how to capture all the potential waffle-eating target market. I would have loved to be in that meeting. "Dammit Phil, we need to get 'em from both directions. Build two of 'em."

One Waffle House was empty, thus proving my theory that they never needed two in the same place. We drove to the next. There were two people sitting in there and some local guys retrieving a to-go order. It looked good, so we committed.

The All-Star Breakfast is the only way to order, in my mind. For seven bucks, you get more ham, eggs, and waffle batter than one man could ever want. It's a training course in economies of scale.

Naturally, the sales guy came out, and I started asking questions.

Waffle House

"Never been to a Waffle House before. What's so great about it?" I launched my opening salvo.

"Nothing like it in the world, sir," replied Michael, our late-shift host.

Michael had been working at Waffle House for thirty years. Yes, thirty years. He wasn't the CEO or a division manager. He was the guy that makes the waffles. Thirty years of making waffles. He'd never moved up into management or even worked his way down the counter to cashier. Michael mans the grill.

I can't even fathom the amount of uneasiness, boredom, or ladder-climbing restlessness I would have felt after about twenty minutes of making waffles. But I immediately respected this guy. He knew who he was and where his skills shined to provide value to the world. He was loyal, and he was not interested in climbing the ladder.

When about eighteen months passes in a corporate role, the unwritten rule is that you better start calculating your next move. It's all about getting to the top and fast. Not for Michael. For Michael, it was about knowing who you are through and through.

This guy had been making waffles and cracking eggs for thirty years, and I don't think there could be a better ambassador to Waffle House than him. No amount of market research, focus groups, and targeted social media strategy could capture the joy of the waffle better than this guy.

We got to talking. He took me through the menu, talked up the hash browns, sold me on a peanut butter waffle, and poured a mean cup of joe. Rosie, who eats like a bird, ordered the whole All-Star just because she was riveted by Michael's brilliant illustration of Waffle House cuisine. Michael was an ambassador.

It continued, and we soaked it up. He broke down the strategy of having a Waffle House on both sides of the highway. He talked about how drunken celebrities come to Waffle House and sometimes get into fights. He tipped us off on how the coffee mugs sell out at Christmas and how social media was loaded with legendary Waffle House stories. Michael was the greatest ambassador to anything I've ever seen. The rest of the world passed this guy off as a short-order cook holding down the late shift. All I saw was a spokesman better than Michael Jordan or Mohammed Ali. Imagine if this guy was selling the faith.

As we were coming to visit Bama, as the locals call it, I asked about things to do in the area.

"Hey Michael, what do you recommend we do in Alabama?"

"Go to Waffle House."

I chuckled. He had fired back without taking a breath.

"No. Go to Waffle House. It wouldn't be right to tell you anything else."

This guy was dropping wisdom on us right and left. I'll say it again. There has never been a greater ambassador for anything, ever, than my man Michael. In his mind, it wouldn't be right to advocate for anything other than Waffle House. It floored me. This guy was pure gold. How in the world did I keep running into these kinds of guys, and why?

I talked Michael out of a free coffee mug, we took some pictures, and hit the road. For the rest of the night, I couldn't shake the idea of this guy. As we rolled down the moonlit highway toward Tuscaloosa, I found myself running back through memory after memory where I could have been an ambassador like Michael. There were times I didn't stand up for colleagues under fire. There were times I didn't stick to principal in meetings because I was playing it safe and political. There were times that I could have mentioned the underlying faith which really drives my viewpoint and decisions.

There were times I could have stood up as people made offhanded comments about Jesus freaks. There were jobs I left when I could have been more loyal.

There was the time a neighbor couple aborted a child because the amnio came back indicating genetic disorder, and I was silent. Ouch.

I know Waffles can be easier to advocate for than complex issues in this world. But the simple fact of the matter is that this guy was steadfast for thirty years. He was clear. He was undeterred.

If Michael was a priest, he could have ended up pope. No question.

* * *

The corporate guy is always faced with the reality that the secular world really doesn't want faith. Somehow, we are all to live in a world where everything is relative, but relativism doesn't work when you have to call balls and strikes. When the chips are down, somebody will rise up and define the strike zone. Somebody always decides what is right and wrong. So, why don't we leave it up to God anymore? That is the ultimate question, I suppose.

Thus, the company man is stuck between playing down his faith while trying to balance the relative, until it's necessary to make a tough call. There's nothing relative in putting your stake in the ground and standing by a decision.

Waffle House

That is what was so interesting about Michael the Waffle House cook. He just flat out knew who he was and what he stood for in life.

* * *

Another great example of steadfast belief is Saint Thomas More. An English lawyer and statesman, More was beheaded on July 6, 1535, in the Tower of London. He was steadfast to the point of the guillotine.

Thomas More was kind of a big deal. He knew how to operate in the boardroom, and he could move and shake with the big boys. He probably hung out in some swanky English pub with all the barristers and high-society elite. More was the kind of guy who would actually own a corduroy smoking jacket.

GQ before moveable type, More could go head to head with the Dos Equis guy in terms of cool. He was so cool that his mom might have had a tattoo that said "Son."

Although he was born into a high-society family, More's skills became sought after as he grew. He was educated at Oxford in law, and in time he would become the right-hand man of King Henry VIII. He was so trusted by the king that More was elevated to lord chancellor, and at one point presided over the entire northern half of England.

More was also steadfast in faith, which became more and more a factor as Henry VIII plowed through wives. As the king drifted away from the Catholic faith, Thomas More was perhaps its greatest defender in England. As their relationship strained, the king asked More to sign a letter to the pope, requesting annulment from his wife Catherine. More refused.

In the end, Thomas More was sent to the guillotine for refusing to sign the Act of Supremacy, which denounced papal authority and established the King of England as the head of what would become the Anglican Church.

Thomas More was steadfast in faith like Michael was steadfast on the Waffle House. His last words were, "The king's good servant, but God's first."

Thomas More paid the ultimate price for being steadfast in the face of relativism. The pope is the head of the church, not the king. For More, sticking to that belief eventually left no room to live under the radar. Eventually, he was exposed and had to claim his true colors.

That is why guys like Thomas More and Michael the Waffle House cook have a leg up on the rest of us. They have already decided where their loyalties fall, and when the chips are down, there is nothing to discuss. They know where the lines of morality and acceptability are in their life. Tough but simple.

Saint Thomas More was canonized in 1935. Michael the Waffle House guy is probably still cracking eggs and dropping excellence just outside of Tuscaloosa.

9

Purity and the Customer

You don't have to look far to find someone who thinks the world is falling apart. Ask a liberal, and they will tell you the gun culture will be our downfall. Ask a conservative, and they'll point immediately to the gender debates. Ask anyone over fifty and, well, all hope is lost given there's no more Saturday morning cartoons.

Think about the shift in culture we've witnessed. Fifteen years ago, getting a girlfriend from an internet dating site was pathetic. Now, your true love comes knocking on your digital device. Cupid has hung up his arrow for a quick swipe left on your iPhone 25. Things have changed for sure, and nobody will argue that modern culture radiates purity.

Virtue is defined as "behavior showing high moral standards." Classic literature is ripe with the virtuous hero taking the high ground to slay the villain. Virtue is long regarded as society's knowledge of right and wrong and its ability to stay on the rails.

There are people everywhere saying these are the worst of times. The lines of acceptability are being blurred. Nobody would argue that premise. Just look at how the corporate dress code has evolved in the professional work environment.

When I started in pharma as a field salesman, it was suit and tie. Even at the national meetings, we dressed professionally. When I was promoted into the home office, jeans were not an option. Within a couple of years, casual Friday slipped past the fashion police into the mainstream. Now, seemingly as a retention tactic for millennial employees who can't tie a Windsor knot, people show up in flip-flops and sweats. Shower optional. To some, it seems like a complete surrender of decorum. Wear a potato sack and an aluminum hat, just get something done, and don't leave until at least four.

But make no mistake, there is virtue in those who show up on a winter day in cargo shorts, wool socks, and a pair of Birk's. Try throwing away an aluminum can in front of these guys. Maybe virtue has just shifted and redefined itself in some sort of secular way. Culture identifies what is important, and those elements drive behavior.

Let's take a quick look at the slippery slope Grandpa complains about as he waxes philosophy on the porch swing.

1. One hundred years ago, if you knocked up your girlfriend, you either got married at the business end of a 12 gauge, or Sandy went away to finishing school.
2. Fifty years ago, the company man was unquestionably loyal to the paycheck.
3. Thirty years ago, you still called anyone who looked like an adult "Mister" or "Missus," and a gentleman always opened the door.
4. Now choose your bathroom, and worship a moose if you want, but for goodness' sake, don't throw away a plastic bottle.

There is certainly virtue out there, but it is no longer anchored in universally recognized moral concrete. The definitions of right and wrong seem to change in real time. Don't get me wrong, recycling is good but so was looking sharp at work and opening doors for the ladies.

* * *

In a recent conversation with a physician who lectures on behalf of our company, I was reminded of how the virtue phenomenon impacts corporate communication. Pharmaceutical companies use physician lecturers as paid speakers to deliver clinical and promotional material on medicines. It makes sense. A medical colleague is a more credible voice than a salesperson to deliver highly clinical information.

All major companies have speaker bureaus that spend millions a year on hundreds of guest lecturers. A good physician speaker can make well over $100,000 a year in speaking engagements. I've managed these types of speaker bureaus for some of the biggest medical brands in the world. To be considered a credible voice for a medicine is a big deal to a physician. The corollary can be drawn with the sports analogy from a few pages back. People want to be with a winner, and they also like to hear from the experts.

Think about it for a second. If you go to the car lot to buy a new ride, you can predict you'll get stuck with Steve the salesman with the slicked-back hair and the awkward high-fives. Never in your life will you weigh the pros and cons of a Toyota with Mario Andretti.

In medicine, it's the opposite. Biopharmaceutical companies find the experts, bring them into program settings, and have them brief potential new users of a medication on how it handles in the turns. So, in an almost literal sense, you are buying from Mario Andretti in the medical setting. You get to hear from the world's foremost experts on a topic before you buy.

Anyway, back to the story.

I was in Denver and found myself discussing upcoming programs with one of our speakers. The conversation drifted to how we invite other physicians to programs. The typical process runs in a grassroots fashion. The local sales reps arrange for a visiting lecturer to fly in from some academic center or larger market. Then those reps deliver printed invitations to the surrounding medical offices and hospitals. The sales reps set up a restaurant as a venue and pay for dinner that is served during the lecture. It's all on the up and up, regarded as standard pharmaceutical marketing practice.

In this case, the physician speaker did not want his name on the invites. What? The speaker was afraid that by having his name on the invitation, it would somehow promote the program and also promote our medicine. I was stunned. I tried to somehow talk through the situation.

"You don't want your name on the invitation?"

"No, it reflects poorly on my practice and suggests I'm biased."

"Well, you have a choice in medicines to prescribe, and if you use our medicine and are willing to speak on behalf of that medicine, then you inherently show that you are willing to endorse the medicine."

"I know, but it can't be in writing."

"What?"

"I'll do the lecture, but keep my name off the invites."

"But it is you the other physicians are coming to see."

"I know. It's crazy."

"But that's like putting on a concert and not putting the name of the band on the flyers."

"I know."

The translation in this case clearly illustrates the cultural virtue phenomenon. The doctor likes and uses our medicine, wants to be paid to speak and be regarded as an expert, but doesn't want anyone to know about it. Discretion and credibility are certainly factors in this case, but to request to be an anonymous yet compensated spokesperson is a new one.

Why are we so afraid to stake a claim on matters of importance? Everyone is playing it safe on the fence. What if Nike had to market Air Jordan as Air Somebody in the NBA?

At times, I think I have a front-row seat to watch the crumbling of common sense. Put all this into the first century. Jesus went around curing people, calming the storms, and commanding a few fish to multiply and feed thousands. He was discrete at times, bold at others, and in many ways was a man of a few words. But people knew he claimed what he stood for.

The leper walked up to Jesus and begged for healing. "If you wish, you can make me clean." "I do will it. Be made clean." (Mark 1:40–41).

The apostles were terrified in the storm. "Teacher, do you not care that we are perishing?" "Quiet! Be still!" (Mark 4:39).

To the deaf man's ears: "Be opened!" (Mark 7:34).

Then at the moment of his brutal death, a Roman centurion, who probably began his day thinking this would be a pretty regular Friday shift, looks up at Jesus and says, "Truly this man was the Son of God." (Mark 15:39).

Think about it. A low-level Roman commander crowns the name of Jesus as God, all the while standing directly in the face of the mob. Jesus knew who he was, and by the time it was over, the guy on the sidelines, who likely hadn't followed much of his ministry, proclaimed he is God. To me, this is just a story that illustrates there is no room on the fence in

Purity and the Customer

Christianity. "So, because you are lukewarm, neither hot nor cold, I will spit you out of my mouth." (Rev 3:16).

Jesus was the expert on miracles, and he claimed every one of them for his Father in heaven. He never took some approach that somehow legitimized all religions or in any way was lukewarm. Nothing sounded anything like corporate babble.

Imagine the Gospels in corporate speak: "Uh ... Jesus here ... I like all religious opinions here and think everything is relevant. All ideas should be on the table and open for laddering up to further exploration. I mean, let's maintain the unbiased position and circle back in another meeting. Okay, let's break into groups and do some team-building trust falls. Careful with your trigger words."

No. He said it clearly. "No one comes to the Father except through me." (John 14:6). He claimed it all the way to the cross. Christ stated his case and then let the chips fall as they would, with no circling back. He was clear and bold with what he wants us to do.

"Go into the whole world and proclaim the gospel to every creature. Whoever believes and is baptized will be saved; whoever does not believe will be condemned." (Mark 16:15–16).

But he wasn't finished.

"These signs will accompany those who believe: in my name they will drive out demons, they will speak new languages. They will pick up serpents [with their hands], and if they drink any deadly thing, it will not harm them. They will lay hands on the sick, and they will recover." (Mark 16:17–18).

Yet we can't as society muster up enough backbone to claim unequivocally that cargo pants are not a good call for work? We can't say clearly that work is good for society, and capable people must pull their weight? We can't articulate that taxes are necessary but stifling tax rates are detrimental? And a lecturer won't actually endorse the topic on which he is paid to lecture. What is happening?

Virtue has been compromised and redefined as personal character traits which are individualistic and moveable. We all want to live comfortably on the fence and never take a stand. Virtue is no longer the behavior reflective of the highest moral standards. Virtue is now the behavior that accepts all standards or no standards.

Thus, as we face a society that is more and more relative, complete with shifting virtue, it is important to remember who had the backbone to take on the entirety of human failing, with almost no resources. Whether we realize it or not, he is the one we are looking for as we seek "me time" at the bar or in hot yoga class. There is one who can lead us out of this mess, and his message is crystal clear.

You want to live your best life? Jesus is the answer.

10

A Cold Walk in Billings

A COLD walk in Billings sounds much more like the chorus line of a country song than a chapter in the long journey to faith. But I've come to learn that if you just exercise your faith, meaning do something simple about it once in a while, divine things will transpire. Business trips are a great proving ground for the faith and the perfect spot for the Holy Spirit to slap you around a bit.

It was early spring, if my memory serves me, and I was on a regular trip to see customers in Montana. The Big Sky swing is a corporate traveler's dream. Of course, I'm saying that tongue in cheek. The ratio of travel-to-customer interaction is about one thousand to one. Flying into town and traversing the state for a couple days of sales calls pencils out as maximum effort for available return.

From my home in Idaho, it takes a whole day to get to Montana. Fly west to go east. When you arrive, there's nothing to do but wait for the next day for appointments. You are sitting in God's country without your skis or your fly rod. You might as well be in Detroit.

Inevitably, a Montana trip might take you from Helena to Gillette, Wyoming, and back to Billings. In case you are counting, that's 944 miles end to end. Montana sales work can put a lot of miles on both you and the truck. Most sales guys turn a company rig (75,000 miles) in less than two years and hit at least one deer in the process.

On one particular trip, I flew into Billings the night before and stayed downtown. The days were packed with long miles between customers. As a manager, my role was always to meet up with the local sales professional and ride shotgun as they worked the route. In my case, our Montana rep was the best of the best. She owned Montana, in the sense that she had won more President's Club sales awards than anyone in the nation. When I visited Montana, I was privileged to work with her. A 900-mile sales trip with an underperforming rep would be enough to make a manager want to jump out of the car and walk home. I was lucky to work with the best.

This story begins with another early morning. It must have been Lent because I was trying to get to daily Mass once in a while. Nonetheless, I got up early and set out on a cold predawn walk to find Saint Patrick's Cathedral. The church is a beautiful stone church first opened in 1904 that shares the seat of the bishop with Great Falls.

* * *

Catholics settled Montana in force over the course of its history. One of the most noteworthy Catholic enclaves in Montana is the mining town of Butte. The town was established in the mid-1800s as a mining camp and ended up being one of the West's biggest boomtowns. The boom came from copper, and the Catholics came from Ireland. Lots of them. The evidence of this time of feast, faith, success, and failure is a ninety-foot statue of Mary high atop the mountain that looks over Butte.

Our Lady of the Rockies, as she is called, sits at an elevation over 8,500 feet, keeping watch over the Butte faithful. The statue was promised by a gentleman who prayed his wife would survive cancer, which she did. As a gift to Butte, the idea of the statue began to take shape. Ultimately, the statue was airlifted in place in December of 1985, commemorating a dedication to Our Lady in Montana.

A Cold Walk in Billings

* * *

Back in Billings, the church I had searched on my phone was about four blocks away. It was cold, dark, and nobody was on the streets. The stillness of the morning hadn't been broken by the first wave of commuters. I walked in near silence. An early morning stroll on quiet streets before a long day of work is great preparation for the mind.

When I arrived at the cathedral, the whole place seemed locked up and dark. That morning, it appeared obvious there would be no morning Mass. I just stood there in the dark with no particular plan and figured I'd just loop my way back to the hotel, hoping to find a coffee shop. It was too early for a cold one, even though it was, in fact, five o' clock in far eastern Europe. Just then an older lady walked up toward the side door of the church. She paused, looked back at me, and invited me inside.

"Come with me," was all that she said. In my mind she had said, "Come with me, you look like you need it."

I couldn't help thinking that my experience in Australia all those years ago was about to happen again. Was this lady an angel? I have no idea, but she appeared to show up out of nowhere. Nonetheless, I joined my new stranger friend, and we settled in a small chapel which was situated just off the main altar. The whole of the church was dark except for one light illuminating this little alcove chapel.

We sat down in silence as a few more ladies showed up, and it was relieving that they did. I was getting nervous, as at this point, I was beginning to think the first lady might actually be an angel, and I had no idea how to make casual conversation with a celestial being.

"So . . . how are things in heaven? Play Bunco with Mary?"

In the end, the crowd topped out at ten. Then my new friend, whose name I still hadn't gotten, pulled a binder out of her handbag. She gestured to me to follow along, so I sat beside her.

We recited morning prayers from the ancient and traditional Divine Office. It was beautiful and brand new to me. As a sidebar, a typical cradle Catholic knows less about the traditions of our great faith than a new convert. I had no idea what we were doing, even though I had sat through a lifetime of Sunday Masses. That little moment in itself was a wakeup call.

Page after page, prayer after prayer, and the whole situation just became more peaceful. It was beautiful. I found myself second-guessing all my decisions in life while simultaneously knowing that this angel that looked like my mother-in-law brought me here to clarify who I needed to be centered around. I ran through all the nights of closing down the bars and all the smaller moments of simply not living into my potential.

I've never robbed a bank or laundered money. I chased a few girls but wasn't great at it. My wife might even say I'm a pretty decent husband. But sin is sin, and it has a way of stacking up and reminding you that your soul needs a pressure-washing once in a while. That peaceful morning was another unscheduled moment of reckoning. Sitting still and soaking up that moment was my only option. There was nowhere to go and no safety call coming to release me from this experience. At this point, I hadn't been to confession in maybe twenty-five years, and it was time to listen up.

"Get serious. I need you," was the message. It was not something audible, but it was clear. "Get serious. I need you."

After about forty minutes of prayers, we gathered our jackets and headed out the door. The older lady stopped me, and we exchanged pleasantries. She let me know that she had been coming to this very spot for years with one request. "I just want my husband to join the church before it's too late," she said with a look of longing. Year over year over year through decades of marriage to the same man, her prayer went unchanged. How could she know so matter of fact that this was her husband's number-one missing piece in his whole life? I'm sure she could have prayed for health, financial concerns, his pending retirement, or that he would stop snoring like a steam engine. Nope. Just that he joined the church. That was enough. That was all that was necessary.

Then she really drilled me.

"Thank you for helping me with that prayer this morning."

Wait, did I hear that right? This lady is thanking me for my assistance? She's on the moon, clearly delusional. I'm the guy that is rolling out of the rack, forcing myself to do something simple, something tiny about my faith after years of going through the motions. I'm trying to do the most basic thing during Lent. She's been committed for years. And she is thanking me.

All I can ascertain from this moment of divine intervention is that sometimes we have no idea what people around us need. Further, in those moments we have no idea how profoundly we can help someone, even though we seem to be doing so little. Unaware during the moment, we might actually be in the exact right place at the exact right time to give someone a shot in the arm and lift them up.

A Cold Walk in Billings

I never got the angel's name. It would be all but impossible to follow up and find out the outcome of the constant vigil she held for her husband. But I have concluded that for some reason, the Holy Spirit granted her one more person at her side that early morning.

That particular corporate trip came and went with forgettable fanfare. I'm sure I said all the right things to the customers and provided stellar coaching to my sales professional. But all I remember is that lady thanking me for praying with her before sunrise.

* * *

As a corporate long-hauler, I've been in conference rooms from LA to Atlanta to Manhattan to KC and back again. One thing for certain about the corporate life is that silent moments are far and few between. Lots of noise, always. Oh, and constant motion. Most days are long, and most nights are short. How are we really ever to expect any rest, not to mention finding five minutes of quiet?

That morning in Billings was almost completely silent but for the prayers. It was early, dark, and beautifully quiet. But I think much of it came down to our location. The Catechism astutely takes up the issue of finding the right location to pray. "The choice of a favorable place is not a matter of indifference for true prayer." (CCC 2691).

Thus, it seems that not only should we know how to pray, we should apparently know where to pray: "The church, the house of God, is the proper place for the liturgical prayer of the parish community." (CCC 2691).

Think about that for a moment. How many Catholics do you know who rarely, if ever, see the inside of a church? I know people who are quick to defend their choice to pray anywhere they choose. Take it further, the Eli Young Band has a great country song called "Saltwater Gospel," where they trade Sunday church for self-worship in the sand, sun, and flip-flops.

But if we dig into the two thousand years of tradition and meaning of our church, we quickly learn that there is in fact a required location for worship and prayer. The Catechism continues to drop its knowledge on us: "The Christian family is the first place of education in prayer." (CCC 2685). Monasteries exist . . . "to further the participation of the faithful in the Liturgy of the Hours and to provide necessary solitude for more intense personal prayer." (CCC 2685).

Location, location, location. Like the lady in Billings, we are called to get out of the rack early and actually go somewhere to pray. Church on

Sundays is the easiest and most nonnegotiable location of prayer. A corner in your home dedicated to prayer and Scripture is another recommendation.

As the resident non-theologian writing this book, I take the simpleton's approach to everything. My analysis is that the world is made for noise, constant noise. Christ, by way of establishing prayer and the Eucharist, literally sets aside a day of the week for us to be quiet. A day of the week to shut down, shut up, sit, and listen. Humanity needs an hour a week of quiet.

I'll take the silence of the location offered and guaranteed by Christ in his church. It's brilliant.

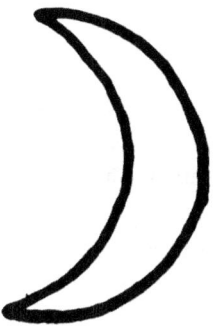

11

Men's Room Confession

There is nothing more demeaning than standing in line to take a dump at an airport. People actually line up outside the stall door to take a warm seat vacated by some dude who just ate the Chinese fried pork in the food court next to gate 35. It's the unspoken reality of connecting through O'Hare.

In the men's room, there is an unspoken, ancient code of behavior. The first rule of business is that one must take all human measures to "sit" only in emergency situations. If a man must sit, the code kicks in as follows:

- Don't ever speak to a man who is down.
- Don't ever look through the crack in the stall door.
- To determine occupancy, look for feet.
- Never make eye contact.
- Try and keep the noise down.
- Last, and critical, leave an empty stall between you and the other guy.

This ancient code may be the most timeless, unwritten, and loyally followed process in the world. But on a late night in an airport full of guys stuck on weather delays, there can be pressure on the system. Literally.

Flights keep coming in, the bars fill up, and the lines start to form. The unease is palpable if you are the unfortunate one who is next in line. The moment of maximum awkwardness comes when the guy you are going to follow meets you face to face at the stall door. No eye contact—for goodness' sakes—no eye contact. Bite your lip, take the warm seat, and get it done.

What in the world does this have to do with religion, God, or anything remotely decent and tasteful? Simple. We can't live without lining up and removing the waste.

Think about it. Four beers, a bowl of chili, and a pile of Terminal 4 curly fries at about 11:47 p.m. after a long day in the corporate rough and tumble is not going to sit well. The human body knows waste and knows that it must get rid of it. Now.

When the waste is gone, the man is cured of all ills. Perhaps temporarily, but make no mistake, the power of removing waste leaves a man at peace.

* * *

Okay, the wages of sin are just like the time bomb of a Newark International chili dog. There is something about our human condition that tells us deep down that we need to eliminate sin. Right and wrong are instilled in our human condition at the most basic level. People know when they are on the wrong side of a decision. The sin piles up and piles up, and it needs to get out or look out.

Enter confession. Why don't we stand in line anymore for confession? Why don't we treat sin with the same urgency as the aftermath of a bad Cobb salad? Why don't we revel in the pure joy of redemption even if we know we have to come right back after the next company meeting?

Confession, reconciliation, and penance are all terms for the church's process to eliminate the nuisance of sin from our daily lives. Most of us are not bank robbers. But we are flawed as human beings, so like it or not, sin is here to stay. The church, by establishing the process of confession, had tremendous insight on the matter long before the existence of the indoor plumbing metaphor. Christ offered humanity the opportunity to eliminate the sin, and we should be more active in that process.

Men's Room Confession

Georgetown University's Center for Applied Research in the Apostolate (CARA) was founded in 1964 to focus on social research to inform decisions within the Catholic Church. According to 2016 data, only 28 percent of Catholics go to confession at least once a year. We go to great lengths to better ourselves physically and find our inner peace, but we shy away from the ultimate gift of peace.

The question is why does it appear that most Catholics doubt the need for this sacrament? One reason could be the Protestant-centered notion that there is no need for forgiveness of sins after people have accepted Christ. His death on the cross paid the ticket once and for all. That's it. One and done. Let's party.

This does not align with the multitude of biblical teachings on the matter. Jesus himself was very clear as he addressed his apostles following the resurrection: "Receive the holy Spirit. Whose sins you forgive are forgiven them, and whose sins you retain are retained." (John 20:22–23).

We seemed to be bound and determined to hold onto our mistakes and disasters, but God makes the benefit of confession crystal clear: "If we acknowledge our sins, he is faithful and just and will forgive our sins and cleanse us from every wrongdoing." (1 John 1:9).

Perhaps it is that simple for the corporate guy. After every corporate meeting that leaves you with a binder of market research you'll never look at again, and a headache from a week in the Marriott lounge, go to confession. Get the waste out.

* * *

Who would ever think of a faith-based book that comes complete with a chapter on bathroom humor? Nobody. But sin is waste, pure and simple, and unless we face the reality of our human inclination to fail, we miss the point.

Humanity's inclination to fall for the trick of sin is addressed brilliantly by Saint Pope John Paul II. During the first five years of his papacy, from 1979 to 1984, he addressed live audiences every Wednesday. All told, there are 129 Wednesday addresses that comprise this teaching, which became known worldwide as the Theology of the Body. A brilliant explanation of sexual ethics and morality, it is best described in the words of the pope himself: "God has a plan for us—a plan for our lives, for our bodies, for our souls, for our future. This plan for us is extremely important—so important that God became man to explain it to us."[1]

One of the key terms unpacked and explained in Theology of the Body is relevant in addressing sin. It is the concept of concupiscence. It's a big fancy word that simply states that all of humanity is inclined to lean toward sin. Think about that for a second. Although we are destined for heaven, given that we persevere in faith, we are slightly leaning toward the train wreck. That tells me I have to always be on my toes, at work or at home.

When I first heard this term, the visual that came to mind is that of a speedometer with a gauge that ranges from zero to one hundred miles per hour. If one hundred is heaven and zero is Dante's Inferno, then humanity, due to this concept of concupiscence, is sitting at about forty-two miles per hour. Yes, we're slightly inclined to look at the hot woman in the coffee shop wearing stretchy pants. But we are also given the strength to resist by way of morality and virtue.

The Catechism takes it all a little deeper. Concupiscence is "the tinder for sin. It is left for us to wrestle with, it cannot harm those who do not consent but manfully resist it by the grace of Jesus Christ." (CCC 1264). Then Timothy brings it home and drops the mic on the issue: "An athlete cannot receive the winner's crown except by competing according to the rules." (2 Tim 2:5).

The Catechism (CCC 1264) goes on regarding our inclination to wreck the train. We are not predestined to come apart at the seams but are rather simply inclined that way ever since Adam and Eve choked down that bad apple. This theological point can easily be proven in any group of men. Walk by a beautiful woman, and watch the neck straining and strategic glances. Next, find any group of women, and you'll certainly hear gossip. We have an inclination to at least be intrigued by the forbidden. The reality of concupiscence in humanity does not mean we don't have the moral fortitude to resist. Again, be on your toes.

The good news is that the Catholic tradition includes a way for us to relieve the chaos of sin by literally talking to someone and getting it all off our chest. Confession is one of those subjects that is either of critical importance to life, or it is cast onto the ash heap of old, worn-out ritual. Every Catholic eventually needs to come to this realization and decide where they stand. That decision is paramount to a healthy Catholic faith.

---

1. Butler and Evert, Life, Love, and the Theology of the Body, 1.

Men's Room Confession

If I remember correctly, in grade school I received my first confession with a priest, and that was it for twenty-five years. Nobody pushed me to go to confession.

My parents never went either, as I recall. Confession just wasn't a topic that was high on anyone's list. Growing up in the 1980s, the church had resorted to "community reconciliation." We'd roll in at the beginning of Lent, and the priest would absolve everyone of their sin with a couple of prayers and some holy water. The gathering lasted maybe an hour. Our family followed it with a race to be first out of the parking lot so we could get a seat at the pizza joint before the rest of the dirty mackerel snappers.

Once I took early retirement from my semiprofessional career in funneling brews, I found myself more curious about faith. Every book I picked up reminded me that there was so much more to learn about faith, sin, and redemption. Nondenominational Christian groups such as Young Life and Campus Crusade were stops along the way. My wife grew up Lutheran. Many of my buddies didn't take faith or church very seriously. I concluded pretty quickly that I would remain Catholic, but I wasn't quite sure why.

Fast forward twenty-five years, my wife converted after twelve years of discernment, and we're still in the pew every Sunday. Our brilliant Catholic faith has settled into my mind as a constant curiosity. I look up every question I cannot answer and have never been skeptical of any element of the faith. So, my conclusion is that our Catholic faith is the truth, and confession is a big element of that truth.

The Catechism is loaded with the theological basis and relevance of confessing one's sins to a priest. This topic in itself could fill thousands of pages, but here's my take on this issue. Life is a train wreck, and we flat out need to admit when we screw up and get it off our chest audibly. We need to tell someone. If you don't come clean on a mistake, it just eats at you. Anyone who's ever stolen their sister's Halloween candy knows this unless they are devoid of a conscience. We have to get the waste of sin out and off our chest. The way to do that is to tell someone, and who better to tell than the stand-in for Christ?

An educated Greek, Tertullian, was renowned as a great lawyer in the ancient empire. He died in about 220 AD. Although he was a well-known scholar and legal mind, his great passion was the defense of the gospel. One of his famous quotes is on how persecution acted to grow the church: "The blood of Christians is seed."[2] This guy was on it, and he also nailed the

---

2. Aquilina, The Fathers of the Church, 91.

definition of penance as "the second plank of salvation after the shipwreck which is the loss of grace." (CCC 1446).

Train wreck. Shipwreck. Now they are speaking my language. The Catechism goes on to say that the "Church is inseparable from reconciliation with God." (CCC 1445). I think this implies that the church cannot remain connected to God as a whole if those of us sitting in the pews on Sunday are not actively trying to dispose of our own shipwrecks. Take it further, we all love to point out the sinister brokenness in the priesthood. It seems to let us off the hook. If those guys are a mess, then I can be also. But if individuals make up the church, then we have a responsibility and are accountable in maintaining its grace and holiness by keeping our own house in order. That'll make you think when you're three bourbons in on a long flight from Philadelphia.

There is good news. For thousands of years, the church has given the barely faithful a procedure for penance. We are to confess our disasters to a priest audibly. We are asked to literally get all the shipwreck that is life off our chest. Say it out loud. It's therapeutic. The priest, contrary to popular secular opinion, is the exact right person with whom to talk. He is ordained in a long line of consecrated teachers that include 266 popes. That lineage draws an unbroken line all the way back to Peter. So, when we confess to a priest, we are talking to Christ himself. I'll take that any day.

The Catechism continues, "All mortal sins of which penitents after a diligent self-examination are conscious must be recounted by them in confession, even if they are most secret." (CCC 1456). Sounds a bit like modern-day personal coaching or counseling. Just get it off your chest. There's no need for a juice cleanse. Just tell the priest, and get it over with already.

The documents from the Council of Trent take it even further: "While therefore the faithful of Christ strive to confess all sins that come to their memory, they no doubt lay all of them before the divine mercy for forgiveness; while those who do otherwise and knowingly conceal certain ones, lay nothing before the divine goodness to be forgiven through the priest; for if one sick be ashamed to make known his wound to the physician, the latter does not remedy what he does not know."[3]

There is a billion-dollar business designed to let all your worries drift away. Take a cruise, do hot yoga, get a couples massage, sit in a hot tub full

---

3. Catholic Church, *Catechism of the Council of Trent*, Session XIV, "Chapter V: Confession."

of mud. If that doesn't work, get an amicable divorce, grab a trophy wife, and spend half the year in Costa Rica posting excellence on Instagram.

Call it what you want. It's sin, and we need to be vigilant, or individuals and our church will drift into the ridiculous. Confession is one of our great weapons against the ongoing shipwreck. Saint Augustine sums up the benefit of confession:

> "Whoever confesses his sins . . . is already working with God. God indicts your sins; if you also indict them, you are joined with God. Man and sinner are, so to speak, two realities: when you hear "man"—this is what God has made; when you hear "sinner"—this is what man himself has made. Destroy what you have made, so that God may save what he has made . . . When you begin to abhor what you have made, it is then that your good works are beginning, since you are accusing yourself of your evil works. The beginning of good works is the confession of evil works. You do the truth and come to the light."[4]

Everyone wants to go to heaven, but like Kenny Chesney sings, "nobody wanna go now." We cannot operate in a world of cultural relativism and be surprised that people are depressed, anxious, and lost. If we as Catholics can bring back the beauty of confession, by each of us individually participating, the word will get out. Imagine the multitudes of lost and wandering folks who could be granted profound peace by eliminating the sin and waste that is piling up year after year.

Humanity is inclined toward the shipwreck, yes. But there is no reason to do away with God's brilliant gift of cleansing and peace that is confession. Think about this the next time you are staring down the front end of a foot-long coney with extra onions on a long layover at O'Hare.

---

4. Catechism of the Catholic Church, 1458.

12

So Goes the Family, So Goes the World

THE Denver airport was packed, but it wasn't even Christmas break. People were all over the place, shuffling back and forth between gates and the Terminal C Starbucks. It was constant motion, about as busy as I've ever seen an airport. Put it this way, when the line for the ladies' room stretches into the terminal, it's certainly busy. But when the line for the men's room spills out into the hallway, then it must be spring break somewhere. Who knowswhat was going on that day in Denver, but it was most unusual. I was just trying to get home.

I was on the tail end of a business trip. It was about 6:30 a.m., and I was in my "get out of town" mode. I had been in the metro area for the week, calling on neurology offices in order to discuss a novel medication. The conversations were fruitful apart from the predictable cynical customer or two that a salesman must always endure.

Most business travelers have a routine, and I am no different: arrive early, get through security, find the gate, get flight status, find breakfast, walk off breakfast, get coffee, get to the gate, hit the restroom, stretch out, and board first. I do it the same way every time, which raises the question: why even try and control a travel situation? Airline travel puts you in a system, similar to a livestock auction, where you literally have zero control over the schedule or the pace of your day. You are the livestock in this situation. Yet somehow, I think I'm in charge if I manage to create and stick to my airport predeparture routine. Ridiculous, really.

The original and famous Stapleton International began serving Denver in 1929 as a small municipal airport. It was seven miles from downtown Denver. Its namesake was Benjamin Stapleton, who was mayor of Denver from 1923 to 1947 except for one term (1931–1935). Stapleton saw the opportunity and future of aviation and wanted to consolidate local aviation around a single facility. The project was placed under the jurisdiction of a guy named Vail, who ran the city's parks and recreation department. In the end, Stapleton International served Colorado for sixty-five years and became the home of United, Frontier, and many other airlines and services. By the time it was closed in 1995, the city had grown around Stapleton International, making it both an annoyance and a convenience for Denver. People had to listen to planes every night until 2:00 a.m. But if you flew in for business, you were ten minutes from downtown.

In 1995, the last flight landed at Stapleton, and the new Denver International Airport was opened way out in Nebraska. Sort of. DIA isn't really in Nebraska, but you can surely reach out and touch a cornhusker from there. I suppose that one hundred years from now, Denver will grow around this airport as well, and then they will move it out to North Dakota or something. But for now, it just feels like flying to Lincoln and then driving back to the front range.

Nobody in Denver will admit it, but the truth is that people are happy it's so far out of town because they don't want to claim it. It's not a good airport. Too much traffic, too many bottlenecks, lines, and trams to endure to get in and out of the place. Okay, to be fair, it's better than Newark, but only by a slim margin.

So, back to working my way through my morning routine. I made it through TSA and breakfast. I found my gate, and after draining a few cups of joe, had moved on to finding a pitstop before boarding. As I walked along the terminal, passing gate after gate, I kept to myself and my own thoughts. I kept thinking that the vibe of the traveler demographic of the day was much more "vacationer" than "corporate weary." Summertime was here, and people were heading to Cabo or Florida for umbrella drinks and the trophy of a blistering sunburn. All I wanted was a restroom and an on-time departure.

As I sauntered through a sea of humanity sporting bro-tanks, flip-flops, and yoga pants, the whole crowd seemed to move in unison. Nobody had to look at each other, but nobody really had to yield either. Crowds are interesting once you start to look at how they behave. There is a certain intelligence about a crowd. Anyway, up ahead there was a sudden break in the graceful flow of the crowd. It wasn't chaos. It didn't feel like an emergency or something critical. It was just a break in the flow.

The people-mover floor escalator kept right on pulling the overweight and aged down the terminal row without interruption, but for those of us in the walking row, something was suddenly parting the crowd to the right and to the left. As I moved closer to the incident, it became obvious that there was some type of obstruction causing the crowd to yield. The closer I came to the incident, the more I wondered. What was it?

It was a poo.

Yes, it was the organic material identified by local dialect as a stool, growler, landmine, or mudslide. Ah, the world suddenly made sense again. People won't open the door for a lady or help a stranded motorist anymore, but they will definitely give way for a pile on the sidewalk.

I yielded to the right and was able to visually confirm, in fact, we were dealing with a poo. It was literally right in the center of the terminal row, and however it got there must have been impressive. Off to the right was a young family down on the ground who appeared to have something to do with the situation. The wife had a baby on the floor and was frantically working her way through what appeared to be the diaper bag. She had a look of horror on her face like nothing I had seen before. She was frantically trying to rectify what appeared to be a nuclear diaper blowout. The source of the hallway obstruction appeared to have been due to a Pampers structural failure. But something didn't make sense. It required more analysis. Procter & Gamble should have sent a crackpot team of pediatric marketers to investigate.

As the pace of the crowd moved me along, I noticed the husband. He was a pathetic mess that only another man with toddlers and infants could understand. The poor bastard was in bad shape. He knelt by the wife, who was attending to the baby and not missing an opportunity to hit him with glances that decades would fail to erase. It wasn't his fault, but in these situations, those types of facts are immaterial. He held fast with one hand on the dog and another on the older toddler. He was trying to comfort the wife, who clearly wanted to vaporize. This poor guy was toast. Any chance of a little romance while the kids were at the Mickey Mouse Club on the Disney Cruise was out, gone. You could see it on his face.

It was chaos for this couple. For the rest of us, it was a tragic and comedic moment where we were happy that we were not them. I couldn't help thinking that none of it made sense. I mean, normally a diaper blowout affects the kid and whoever is holding her. It must be a one-in-a-million chance that the diaper contents would ever escape and free fall to the floor. Right? Think of the physics involved for that to happen. Or it could have been the dog? Did the mom stop to change the baby, which made Sparky the black lab think he had the green light to let loose? It's a riddle that may never be solved.

Regardless of the source of the problem, it was a pure Chesterton moment, whose quote from his book *Manalive* nails it: "Marriage is a duel to the death which no man of honor should decline."

I digress. Most people just walked by and ignored the mayhem. Most of the passersby had likely been there, done that and had a flight to catch. Nobody wanted to relive a parenting moment like that for another second. So, the sea of people kept moving along, braking right and left, making way for that family to deal with the landmine on their own. Nobody stopped, and everyone went on with their lives. As I passed by, I looked back perhaps for one last glance in solidarity for that husband. I kept thinking to myself, "You work for years to go on a big vacation, and it ends up in a pile of crap." Then right as I was to look away from them for the last time, the wife said something inaudible to the husband, and he literally burst into action and dove to pick up the pile of poo, barehanded. He was in it to win it and he acted. He dove into the situation to save it at the request of his spouse. No Lysol, no gloves, no questions asked. It was real, raw, authentic love in motion.

Then I started looking below the surface, and it made me think. As I looked a little deeper in that moment, I would argue that you could see two saints showing us how to properly do battle with the world. The world just passed right by a family in crisis, but these folks were teaching us all something profound. Sure, the problem would ultimately be solved with little more than some disinfectant and a few ounces of embarrassment, but this little crisis was showcasing something brilliant that the world so desperately desires. Was that family completely invisible, or were they flat out showing us how to save the world?

* * *

Well, it just so happens that Saint Pope John Paul II has something to say about this situation. On November 30, 1986, he was on a nationwide tour of Australia. During his stop in Perth, the capital city of Western Australia, the pope addressed the first Sunday of Advent. He focused squarely on the family. The text of his homily includes the following remark: "As the family goes, so goes the nation, and so goes the whole world in which we live."[1]

There it is. Eighteen words, and you have all you need to take on the world.

This boils down everything that could be seen that morning in the Denver Airport. People moving about, yielding for a family in distress but not assisting. I doubt many thought of the divine nature of the moment. This little family was teaching us perhaps the greatest lesson in all of humanity in that moment. Circle the wagons; family is everything.

Think about it step by step. The situation had gone to crap, literally. The husband and wife hunker down with the kids and start working the solution. The poo may have come from the dog or the baby, either way, they were literally being overrun by humanity, but they held their ground together. Sure, there were emotions and frustration. Who cares? The wife had the baby and the diaper, the husband had the toddler and the dog. Somebody had to act to remove the obstruction in order for the proper, normal flow of humanity to return to Terminal C. Who acted? The family. Did some other passerby grab the poo to clear the path and save the day? No. Was the airport authority on the scene? Not yet. The husband dove into action without consideration of anything, much less his dignity.

That family was schooling Terminal C on just how to save the world. Commit, circle the wagons, hold together, and act.

Life goes off the rails. Jobs fall apart, kids get into trouble, wives and husbands fall in and out of love, politicians ruin economies or cause wars, and the earth just keeps rotating. But in order to get all these elements of life back on the rails, the family is the critical element. Very few people will stop and help, but a family will circle up and take the bullets. They might bitch and moan their way through it, but they will act. The family is the single

---

1. Pope John Paul II, "Apostolic Pilgrimage," https://www.vatican.va/content/john-paul-ii/en/homilies/1986/documents/hf_jp-ii_hom_19861130_perth-australia.html.

most powerful element of humanity. Period. It can literally make the world yield while it protects and nurtures the most vulnerable. No government on earth is as powerful as one tiny little family. Of course a government can wield power and force control, but it cannot nurture and love.

The pope continued his remarks that day in Australia to note that the family is "an indissoluble communion that 'sinks its roots in the natural complementarity that exists between man and woman, and is nurtured through the personal willingness of the spouses to share their entire life project, what they have and what they are.'"[2]

In my words, the view of a simple company man, the pope said something historic that Sunday in Perth. He put the world on notice. He called governments to account. He told the powerbrokers, in no uncertain terms, that a committed husband and wife are unstoppable.

Oh, and I think it was the dog.

---

2. Pope John Paul II, "Apostolic Pilgrimage," para. 7, 14.

13

Me Against the Lizard

SELLING life insurance blows. That's it. What else can you say? I mean, you have to call one hundred people to get ten appointments to get one sale. I don't even know one hundred people I could call in order to allow ninety-nine of them the pleasure of rejecting me. Insurance is certainly necessary, but selling term-life policies to chain smokers in the bar at the municipal golf course is an art in itself.

People can be trained how to sell real estate and medical devices. You have to be born to sell insurance. There are guys out there who seem to have some sort of "competitive salesman" genetic material, and they are the ones who can't get enough of selling copiers, insurance, or vacuum cleaners. They want to be number one and won't stop until they are on top of the leaderboard. It's like these guys are born with one of those big, oversized #1 foam fingers on one hand.

The rest of us might try that kind of selling for a while if we're out of any and all other options. We promptly fail and then get on with living. I did just that, and it turned out to be quite the lesson.

* * *

Before we dive into another story of corporate chaos, it might be worth going back to what our faith teaches regarding work. The letters to the Thessalonians might be a good place to start. Both letters are written by Paul and are explicit in lining out corrective measures the newly faithful need to take in order to stay on the rails. In chapter 3, Paul talks about working hard, pulling your weight, and being careful not to be idle: "If anyone was unwilling to work, neither should that one eat." (2 Thess 3:10).

I don't know about you, but I don't need the Bible to tell me that little nugget of wisdom. My old man was plenty effective on the topic of work, especially on Saturday morning when the grass needed to be cut and my brother was busy sleeping until 11:00 a.m.

The Catechism goes on to say that "work is a duty" (CCC 2427) and that "work is for man, not man for work." (CCC 2428). In other words, as difficult as some job experiences can be, I suppose the message is that we keep going, keep hustling, and keep building. There is value and self-worth in the grind.

It would be wonderful if God would simply put all of us in the perfect situation, where we perfectly fit into the job, the boss is great, and we're all overpaid. We all know it doesn't work that way, but we also forget the value we gain from the rough and tumble of our economic initiative.

> "Everyone has the right of economic initiative; everyone should make legitimate use of his talents to contribute to the abundance that will benefit all and to harvest the just fruits of his labor. He should seek to observe regulations issued by legitimate authority for the sake of the common good."[1]

The simple translation here is that we are supposed to hustle, and it's quite acceptable to build wealth. But we are called to play by the rules. We are to be generous all along the journey, not simply at the end when we're standing over our pot of gold with nothing left to decide other than which tropical port to have the crew throw our ashes off the stern of the family yacht.

---

1. *Catechism of the Catholic Church*, 2429.

The Catholic Company Man

* * *

Somewhere about year ten of my pharmaceutical career, I was on a roll. We had moved to Phoenix and were off and running on a director-level career track. The corporate powers that be were assuring me that I was senior leadership material. They were telling me, via leaked information from top-secret boardroom sessions, that I was in the upper crest of up-and-comers. The corner office was going to be mine as long as I said and did everything correctly for the next twenty years. I was on a rocket ride to the top if I spoke in perfect, emotionally acceptable, non-offensive, situationally appropriate corporate language and never made a mistake. I don't even know what that means anymore, but back then it was addicting to be told you could be somebody someday. Isn't that a Travis Tritt song?

We had baby number four, bought a house with a pool, real estate values seemed to be rising, and we were rolling along. I was what they called a business center leader, helping to manage our downtown Phoenix corporate offices. It was a great gig. The decision-making power was addicting. I mean, it was my sole decision on which toilet paper to buy for the office.

Then the political and financial turmoil of 2008 hit and hit hard. We lived in the epicenter of the national housing crisis and had bought at the absolute top of the market. To pile on, we drove a Suburban, which is the ultimate rig for the good times. Gas prices jumped to over four bucks overnight, and I actually found myself trying to master the art of hypermiling, which at the time was a fancy term for rolling through stop signs and trying to coast around town in order save fuel.

It seemed like it all happened out of the blue, but the warning signals of economic bubbles were shouting at Americans for ten years in advance, yet nobody noticed. They were all distracted by the exploding microbrew fad and that incredible new iPhone that only had one button on it. It was 2008, and all was well until it wasn't.

Of course, when it did hit, everyone thought it would blow over and that in no time we would be back to pounding expensive IPAs poolside in Tempe. But it wasn't to be. Within short order, the economic situation knocked on our company doors, and layoffs were imminent. I was offered an option, which frankly was quite generous. There were too many of us in Phoenix, so they offered to pay for our relocation to move us to an open slot in Portland, Oregon. It's important to note here that corporations are easy to make fun of in a lot of ways, but they can also be extremely thoughtful and generous at times. They could have easily laid us off in Phoenix, with our massive mortgage and equally massive environmentally inappropriate Chevy Suburban, in the middle of the biggest economic crisis in memory. But the corporate heads didn't. They found an out for us, and we took it.

Fast forward, we ended up in Portland for about a year when a great opportunity presented itself. Or so we thought.

* * *

It was too good to be true. My wife, Heather, had grown up in a classic farming town of two thousand people in eastern Washington called Colfax. The area is known as the Palouse, and farmers there yield one hundred bushels an acre of dryland wheat pretty consistently. It is a special place, but unless you have three thousand acres that your family homesteaded on five generations ago, jobs can be tough to find.

Since we didn't have any land or a tractor, and given that Pfizer or Lilly had no plans on opening headquarters in a town without an airport, much less a Dave & Buster's, we figured it was a pipe dream at best to ever live in that part of the world.

Then something divine happened. At least I think it was divine. What we thought Colfax was and what it turned out to be were two vastly different things. But we learned, and perhaps that is what God wanted. Perhaps he needed to fine-tune us a bit.

One day at a fifth-grade girls' basketball game, I ran into a guy, and we got to talking. One thing led to another, and it turned out he was the district manager for a major insurance company. I'll spare you the name, but just know that this guy represented one of those companies who advertise relentlessly during NFL games. He knew that the agency in Colfax was about to turn over. The local agent was retiring, and they were shopping for new blood. They wanted someone young and professional to take on the agency, the lease, the policies, and the staff. It was turnkey.

Almost immediately, I went from the pharmaceutical guy who barely survived a major layoff to being able to bring my wife and kids back to her hometown. I was a hero. My mother-in-law was so happy she couldn't see straight. I just needed to figure out if the opportunity was real and if it all penciled out. I did as much due diligence as I could. I tried to match up the population of the county with the number of insurance carriers who had local offices. I calculated the amount of premium I would have to generate in order to make \$50,000, \$80,000, \$100,000, and so on. We tried to negotiate the most advantageous entry point in terms of taking on the building lease. I was on it and did my very best to make sure all the dots connected.

In the end, we took the leap. We left our corporate career and opened our little storefront on Main Street, USA. We moved to Colfax and made the mother-in-law the happiest lady in the quilt group. I joined the Rotary and got involved in all kinds of local activities. We jumped in at Saint Patrick's Catholic Church and began teaching religious education. Some guy even asked me to join the Masons. Good thing I had heard somewhere that the Masons were not exactly the place for a Catholic, so I passed on that one. Our new business was awesome. For about two months.

Remember when I said there was an art to selling insurance? It's a funny human interaction that takes place when trying to sell something to someone who knows he needs it but doesn't want it. Selling the fourth round of margaritas on a catamaran off the coast of Cabo is easy. Selling life insurance to a thirty-year-old is literally like trying to pry the money out of the cruise budget, and all that does is keep your potential customer from ever meeting José the bartender on that catamaran.

Insurance is awkward and intrusive and unnerving. Think about it. The agent generally comes to your house, lays out fifty pages of paperwork that even a lawyer can't decipher, and then proceeds to assess your propensity for driving poorly, your risk of burning down the house, or your chances of having a coronary before you even get to round one with José the bartender.

All that, and I wasn't half bad at the insurance business. It took some getting used to, but once Heather and I had the staff turned over and had been through the customer list once or twice, we felt pretty good. I learned that I wasn't very talented in the cold-calling department, but there are other ways to engage customers. In fact, cold calling literally made me want to vomit. I just couldn't do it. So to adjust, we shifted our strategy to become as visible in town as possible. As noted above, I joined all kinds of groups, and we even volunteered and ran the community kiddy soccer league for a couple of years. I coached, refereed, painted field lines, you name it. We did almost anything to avoid cold calling people and attempting to convince them I was better than that damn Geico lizard.

* * *

While cleaning up the agency, we found a trail of evidence that suggested the previous agent was less than detail-oriented, and that is being generous.

Me Against the Lizard

At minimum, we knew we had policies and paperwork needing attention. At the worst, there were some customers who thought they had coverage but really didn't, and it wasn't entirely clear where the years of cash they had been paying on premiums had gone. I can remember one phone call like it was five minutes ago. As I sat in my office, I could only hear one side of the conversation, but it was enough to sound the alarm.

"Hello, Colfax Insurance, this is Heather, how can I help you? Yes. Yes. Sure, Mr. Halsenberg, let me go grab your file."

That right there—go grab your file—should tell you something. This place was handed to us with about half of the policies in the computer system and about half in binders and drawers. If you ever hire a corporate consultant with a fancy MBA to assess an opportunity and they miss that little red flag, you probably should not pay them. I digress.

"Thanks for waiting Mr. Halsenberg. Is there another name your policies might be under? As you know, we just took over the agency, and we're learning the ropes around here.

"Yes, uh, of course. No, I don't mean to upset you. I know you are a major landowner here, and your operation is significant in size and that you have a lot to lose and a lot to insure.

"Yes, sir. Can I call you back in ten minutes?"

"I know. I know. Ten minutes. Not a second longer. Yes, sir."

And that's how it started. Ten minutes later after a phone call to the district offices, it was clear that we not only had no files for this farmer's account, but he did not have any policies with our business . . . and he thought he did. He also had the payment records. Wow. After that, we started digging through every piece of paper in that building, literally. We had to find, resort, rewrite, uncover, and decipher multiple customer accounts and put them back together. Fortunately, we didn't lose many of those customers. I think they just saw the concern in our faces and the effort we went through to help repair everything.

To say the least, all the due diligence in the world would never have uncovered this situation prior to us quitting the job, where I was on the "short list" and signing on to sort out a major small business tsunami. But we were committed, and people we didn't even know were counting on us.

* * *

The story of a guy and his wife selling insurance is hardly unique or sexy, no matter how you tell it. But God was clearly doing something with us in this time of chaos. The *Catechism*, in the same section where it addresses employment, talks about the development of the human being: "True development concerns the whole man. It is concerned with increasing each person's ability to respond to his vocation and hence to God's call." (CCC 2461). In this case, there were so many little things to attend to and fix, that it seems we were learning the power of just helping in the moment.

I can't recall any deep theological treatise that ever extolled the virtues of the insurance salesman, but if we didn't clean that place up, then more disorganization, uncovered claims, and general misery would certainly have come to people. God was developing us for sure. And perhaps that development included learning how to see the need of the moment, roll up your sleeves, and just get done what is in front of you without checking your contract value first. Just get to work.

Saint Gregory the Great goes on to summarize for us here: "When we attend to the needs of those in want, we give them what is theirs, not ours. More than performing works of mercy, we are paying a debt of justice." (CCC 2446).

Imagine just for a moment if any conference room in every corporation had one guy who was solely focused on attending to others' needs and giving to their colleagues what is "theirs, not ours."

* * *

We lasted one year as the friendly, small-town insurance agency. I sold lots of policies and at one point was number one in the nation for life insurance sales. We were proud of what we were building, but we couldn't keep up. We had no second income. We took zero salary and barely stayed afloat while both Heather and I worked to clean up the mess. The national agency took $.60 of every dollar of premium (as our purchase agreement stated) while we drowned in overhead and ten-hour days of just trying to get all the existing customers straightened out. We could hardly cover the rent but found a way to pay both the staff and all the bills. It was things like buying groceries that were always in jeopardy.

But it wasn't just lack of income that took a toll. We had people scream at us at the front door, run us down to complain while we were pumping gas, and leave angry, nasty messages on Christmas Eve. I mean, think about it. There's no better time to verbally abuse your insurance guy than on the eve of our Savior's birth.

Once I even had to tell a nice old lady, whose husband had passed away, that he only had a small amount of life insurance, and it was taken out on her, not him. So, there she stood completely broke in my office. Unreal. We did our best, but in the end we had walked into a serious problem and were drowning. It was a glimpse into humanity in its most emotionally raw moments.

And then out of the blue, I got a phone call. Literally, out of the blue. It was a call to come work at Teva Pharmaceuticals as a regional manager in their Multiple Sclerosis division. It was a miracle. We were lost. We were broke and both working frantically to survive. We had moved to a little town in the middle nowhere, which is not exactly where corporate jobs pop up. We had no idea what was to come of our situation. Then boom, one phone call, and we were back on our feet. It was beautiful.

* * *

Big deal. A guy quits a job, then starts his own business, fails, and at some point, gets back on his feet. It's not exactly the first time this story has been told. Supposedly, Abraham Lincoln failed a few times before getting elected to office, and his story is more noteworthy than mine.

The real quest is to find the divine in these moments. I'm using my stories to illustrate the point that God works in all of us, and sometimes we can actually see it unfolding. If you are reading this and have a corner office in some big company or a little shop like my insurance agency, at some point you will be able to relate. There will be moments where we all have a choice to look at life as being directed by God or simply being adrift and guided by nothing. How we choose to look at life in that moment is how we ultimately choose our place in the afterlife. Think about that for a moment. If we see God, he sees us. If we don't, he can't help us. It's a deep yet simple theological concept called free will. God allows us to make the call whether we see him or ignore him.

I like to think my life has some design and meaning to it. After fifty-three years of tripping over myself, I can now see God in almost everything. And when we see him, that is when we must dig into the *Catechism* and finally learn the history, scripture, and tradition. We must galvanize our faith at some point. We are under too much assault to leave our kettle of faith just sitting on the back burner on lukewarm.

My experience in insurance gave me an opportunity to see God like I'd never seen him. I met him via the Holy Spirit in the young seminarian on the Australian beach. I met him in the cabbie that morning in California. And I certainly met God in that Alabama Waffle House in the middle of the night. In this case, however, I met God over the period of a year in a whole lot of broken people, myself being one of them. I met him not in some spellbinding beautiful rainbow but rather in a whole lot of ugly chaos. I can tell you that my Catholic faith would not be nearly as strong as it has become without the failure of that business endeavor.

God found a very unusual way to put us on Main Street in Colfax, Washington, at a perfect moment. Of course, I had no idea of any of this at the time, which is the benefit of hindsight. But indulge me through this reflection. First, God got us there by taking us from Phoenix to Portland to meet some random guy at a fifth-grade sports event.

I would have never looked for an insurance agency, and it dropped in our lap. Somewhere in the Bible, it says "Seek, and ye shall find." Well, we found it without much seeking. It all just happened. Too random to be anything less than divine.

Our year in Colfax produced a harvest personally and spiritually. The customers needed help, and we ministered to them by finding answers. Sometimes they were irate, sometimes confused, and certainly sometimes they were just fine. Regardless of their disposition, they still needed our help. Dealing with customers who need help is a ministry in itself, and we had to learn that in order to see the world as God needed. We had to learn how to actually communicate complicated information to people who had been emotionally hijacked by difficult life events. It was great training for what was to come in life.

Heather and I also found ourselves playing music at church. We had never taught religious education before, but people asked, and we said yes. Small towns are generally not long on volunteers, so it seemed we were just warm bodies. But I'm not so sure. Via that experience, we started to feel like our teaching was not deep enough, and our faith needed study and introspection. The kids wanted more, and we needed more. Plus, the traditional Catholics would not send their kids to our classes, as we were "not Catholic enough" to be considered acceptable to teach. This floored us and pushed us into learning the *Catechism*, more about key saints and Doctors of the Church, as well as really being mindful that what we taught actually aligned with Scripture and Tradition.

As our church involvement grew and our little business started working, my wife grew increasingly disenchanted with the local elementary school. The kids were doing great in terms of grades, but they weren't learning much. Heather is a detail-oriented stickler for high educational standards, with a master's degree in teaching. About the third time she went into the principal's office to light him up over the lack of academic rigor in the school, I knew our insurance agency might have trouble keeping customers. In a small town, you have to tread lightly if you are a business owner, or people will punish you. Lesson learned, but God was at work in the chaos.

The school experience grew into searching for alternatives, which we found in a local Christian school about thirty miles away. There was no Catholic school within about eighty miles, so this little classical academy was our only hope after Heather burned up her welcome with the school principal. Anyway, it turned out that this little classic school had a bit of a Calvinist, anti-Catholic bend to it, so what did we do? We enrolled. In no time, we were commuting sixty miles a day, where we found our kids immersed in Latin, logic, and rhetoric. It didn't take long for the local public school community to jack up the gossip machine and dirty our name. Oh, and I was still trying to show up at Rotary and act like a big supporter of the town. God kept up the work in the chaos because what we found in that school proved to be everything we needed.

Fast forward, our two oldest have graduated from there and have gone on to excel at major universities. More importantly, they learned in no uncertain terms how to spot the Protestant challenge and defend our faith with fact, Scripture, and grace. Every time our kids brought home a question about sola Scriptura or something that ridiculed the papacy, we dove into the *Catechism* and the Bible. We learned Catholic apologetics not as a hobby but as a necessity.

I am convinced that the entire insurance experience was to bring us to our knees, challenge our faith to its core, and set us up for being called to big things in the name of God. Colfax was a divine destination.

If you are keeping score, the chart looks something like this:

1. We leave pharma.
2. God brings us to town with great promise of a business.
3. The business is an immediate mess.
4. We hire new staff and try to pay fairly.
5. We save people who literally have had no insurance for years.

6. The parish needs us for catechism class, so we jump in.
7. The local school is in disarray, and Heather pushes on them to improve.
8. God finds us a classical school and challenges our faith like no other.
9. The national agency is taking $.60 on every dollar we make, and we can't make ends meet.
10. We make literally zero ($.00).
11. As we try and negotiate a new compensation deal with the national company, they lock us out of the agency and send us to collections.
12. As we bounce off rock bottom, the phone rings.
13. Teva calls, and God puts us right back in pharma at the same level we were a year earlier.

Again, so what? I don't think Peter or Matthew would have been very effective if they continued to be preoccupied with fishing or collecting taxes. Those guys were called right off the job, dropped everything, and followed Christ right to the cross. Maybe my little story here just illustrates that even in small ways, God calls us in particular moments to drop everything and get something done for him. Jesus talked frequently about how people would not understand immediately, but they would understand over time. There are dozens of New Testament examples of Jesus preaching parables to the crowds where he has to stop and acknowledge that many in the crowd don't get it. "Why do you not understand what I am saying? Because you cannot bear to hear my word." (John 8:43).

We are human. It takes a while for concepts to sink in through all the Instagram and Twitter residue. We shouldn't be surprised. I guess this was one of those moments for us.

On the surface, our little insurance project was a disastrous career move followed by a failed effort at entrepreneurship. But taking a deeper look, the whole thing looks like a bunch of little moments where God just needed someone to get involved and help clean up a mess. If that was his will, so be it. I'm glad we answered the call.

* * *

In the end, the agency was transferred to a new agent. Our staff member kept her job and was employed all the way through a long terminal illness that eventually took her husband. The new agent got a much better financial deal than we did, and he was successful. The policies were cleaned up, and no paperwork was left in disarray. The little soccer league thrived, and we ended up getting the Teva job right about the moment when we became desperate.

All in all, the crazy experiment worked.

I think all of us can and should look at the decisions and experiences in our lives and determine where God was working in our favor. In this case, for some reason via a wild year of chaos, God got us where he wanted us and got us focused on church to a level we had never considered. There was a window of one year that he needed from me, and afterward, he literally put me right back where I left off. He took our livelihood, and when we were done, he left us in better shape. If I had stayed in pharma and never taken that risk, I don't know if I would have ever experienced the jolt in faith that was necessary to wake up.

14

Trashin' Hotel Rooms

EVERY single man who ever had a corporate job would rather be a rockstar. Anyone who says otherwise is lying. Just the idea of livin' large on a tour bus and playing gigs all over the world outweighs any and all corporate achievement. Maybe a bit of that longing for the big time plays into why so many marketing groups use celebrity endorsement to sell their products. Michael Jordan sold a lot of shoes on his name, to be sure. But don't forget the cool factor that followed the Nike marketing guys who lived a bit of a double life in Michael's corporate entourage. Personally, I wish I was the marketer with Miller Lite when they were making those classic 1980s beer commercials with Bob Uecker.

As a commercial marketer, there is just nothing cooler than working in the celebrity promotion world. If the boss puts you on an endorsement project, it generally means you've earned a bit of a break from market research and compliance meetings. It's a glimpse into the rarified air of the big time. You find yourself hanging out with the coolest people in the world, and those people listen to you while the team strategically folds their celebrity nature into the brand. It's an incredible experience, of which I only had a small taste of over the years. But my little taste of celebrity came complete with its own wild stories. My favorite memory is the quintessential "big party in the hotel suite after the concert" story, and it's a beauty.

My boss and I were in Dallas for a convention of nurses who specialize in treating multiple sclerosis. Attendees came in from all over the world for their annual week of scientific updates. They were always a fun crowd who, during the day, worked hard to learn more about this critical world of patient care. Come cocktail hour, it was a party, and companies on site promoting their products always made the attempt to show everyone a good time. My company was no different, and we had the celebrity edge.

Our celebrity spokesman was a country singer named Clay Walker. You may have heard of him, as he's only sold upward of ten million records. Since his first hit, Clay has logged thirty-one charted singles, eleven number-one songs, and four platinum albums. He's a star and one of the hardest-working performers anywhere. Clay is a great guy. He was stricken with MS at a young age, and he had always worked with us to advance the message of our medicines. He went public with his diagnosis in 1996, and ever since, he has been a spectacular advocate for patients.

We invited him to perform at the nurses conference, and I was in charge of the particulars. The management of a major medical conference is not a small endeavor. The role of conference lead in a corporation normally falls on someone in marketing. In my case, I was one of twelve people in charge of marketing for one of the most important and successful MS medications in history. We ran the brand with less people supporting marketing than a company like Pfizer would deploy, yet our brand generated annual global sales in the billions. That being said, in our shop, the responsibilities of running a medical conference always fell on one person.

Every convention was a monumental undertaking, and I was in charge of three or four big events each year. It was my responsibility to figure out how to get a large corporate contingent into a major city; house them, feed them, book meetings, manage customer events, deal with the unions, schedule the sales group to man the promotional booth, and generally make sure we generate something in terms of positive promotion for the effort. During my time in marketing I managed international conferences in Boston, Copenhagen, London, Philadelphia, Dallas, San Diego, and I'm sure I ended up in Indianapolis along the way.

The complex game of marketing a major medical convention is really a three-fold effort. The goal is to promote your medications, connect with your customers, and keep watch on the competition. Our team for such an event would consist of between fifty to eighty people, who all fanned out to cover every aspect of the event. The medical guys paid attention to the scientific presentations, sales worked the booth, and the marketers keep it all running. No matter your area of expertise, the ultimate goal was maximizing face time with customers, and it was all on the up and up.

At this particular event, we were in Dallas, launching a new dosing indication for our medication, which gave us new things to talk about and a reason to spend a little more money to put on our show. Conventioneering is always better when you have something new to discuss regarding your products. The guys selling the same drug eighteen years into its patent are always bored at those shows.

Anyway, back to the story. Our boy Clay Walker was billed as a nurse appreciation concert, and that it was for sure. This guy can sing and is the ultimate showman. Everything was proceeding smoothly as he delivered his hits "Live, Laugh, Love" and "If I Could Make a Living." The show was private, but it went off like a night at Madison Square Garden.

I was standing near the back of the venue when my phone vibrates, indicating that somebody wanted something immediately. It was my boss from the front row, texting the following: "Clay wants to get together after the show. Set it up." Whoa. Needless to say, I sprang into action, as I'm sure our country phenom was only contracted to sing about five or six more songs. Now, you can't have a get-together with a famous guy in the Marriott lobby bar without the wheels coming off the situation in no time. You need a private spot. So, I leapt into action with absolutely no idea how to pull off an after-party for a major star in six tunes or less. Luckily, I had a suite on the top floor of the hotel that would have to do the trick.

I ran up to my room, scooped up all my socks, underwear, and work junk that had accumulated all over the place, and threw it into the bedroom and closed the door. I called down to catering and had them run up multiple orders of every appetizer item on the late-night menu. The bar ran up a tub of Shiner Bock beers while the sommelier from the restaurant laid in some highbrow wine. I went from zero to ready to rock the twelfth floor of the Renaissance Dallas Hotel in fifteen minutes flat. My boss was texting the whole time with the directive that if it ain't ready, the big star ain't coming up.

Trashin' Hotel Rooms

"Giddy up," I texted back. "All set."

From the time Clay and his band showed up, it was about thirty-five seconds until the rest of the hotel figured out the ruse. My boss evidently got so excited about the concert and all of it that he pretty much told the whole half-drunk nursing world where he was headed with their heart-throb. My room.

If I was twenty-five and on spring break, I would have been into the brews and fired up that a big star was going to invite a hundred of his buddies up to trash my room. It would have been a party badge of excellence that I would wear with pride. But in this situation I was working, and now the party had to be great, it had to rock, and it had to run until Clay and the company executives wanted to close up shop. In other words, I was on the hook. I was the bouncer, the door man, the keg master, and the lone sentinel in charge of holding off the cops. Did I mention that I weigh 175 pounds soaking wet?

The room filled up beyond capacity, and people were having a great time. People were crushing brews and choking down my hastily ordered room service chicken wings. The whole band was there, regaling us with stories of the road. Our company executives were acting like they were the cool kids they had never gotten to be, and Clay was greasing the skids for more product spokesman opportunities. It was a pretty sweet situation until the knock on the door at about 2:00 a.m.

"Hey, Meyer, the cops are here."

So, I headed to the door and was promptly invited, by one of Dallas's finest, to get a handle on the chaos ASAP. The look on the policeman's face was priceless, almost like he would rather be dealing with real crime than babysitting overpaid middle-aged corporate guys trying to act out a rock and roll fantasy. We were just a bunch of harmless fools making too much noise. But it was my room, and I was the one in trouble, so I did my best to negotiate.

"Uh, officer, I have a famous guy in here with his whole band. I'm not sure the problem is solved if I kick this whole mob out of here and they spill down the elevators into the lobby, dragging along a guy who's sold ten million records."

"Don't care, shut it down."

"Roger that, officer."

So, I grabbed another beer and tried to think fast. I walked over to my boss and discreetly informed him that we needed to deal with the cops.

He, in no uncertain terms, told me the party would not be shut down and that it was up to me to deal with the authorities. Understood. I went back to the cop and tried to discreetly tell him that my boss wanted to party, and since he was my boss, I had no say in the matter. Much to my chagrin, the policeman's response was the same: "Shut it down."

Interestingly, the policeman never came into the room. He was dealing with me, and I was to deal with the chaos. I had to address the situation head-on. Nobody was going to make it easy.

I grabbed yet another beer and tried to think even quicker. Pulling a chair out from under the dining table, I jumped up, and towering over the crowd, started shouting for attention. Ignored for what felt like a lifetime, the crowd finally acknowledged I had the floor, but the corner I was painted into was offering no escape option. The cops were saying to shut it down, while the guys who signed my paycheck were explicitly ordering that the party roll without disruption. Thinking back on the moment, I'm not sure how my expensive MBA was relevant. It was one of those moments where you couldn't write it if you tried.

I yelled in my best authoritarian yet HR-acceptable tone: "Everyone! Everyone! Thank you for a great night. Clay, great concert, so glad to have you entertain the troops tonight. Awesome job."

Cheers from the crowd as they raised their drinks.

"I have an announcement," I said, knowing I was going to get thrashed. What kind of moron tries to tell a rockstar to close up an after-party? "A gentleman from the Dallas PD is out front, and he has requested we shut down the festivities for the night, so let's pack it in and shut it down. Again, Clay, awesome show."

Silence. The executives just looked at me with something other than a "you're promoted" facial expression. Then, just like a rockstar, Clay jumps up and yells, "I say . . . we party!" Great chess move. If I was famous, I would have done the exact same thing.

Needless to say, the crowd went wild, and the noise ramped back up like a DJ spinning up a record. And just like that, I headed toward the door, defeated in round one, to face my reckoning with the police officer. At that point, he was becoming amused by my predicament. On my way to the front door, I stopped at the ice bucket for yet another cold one, hoping the solution would be buried somewhere in those twelve ounces.

I walked back to the door, and the police officer just looked at me and shook his head. "Your parents proud of you?"

"No, sir."

"Didn't think so. Now get at least half of these people out right now, or I kick you and everyone out of this hotel."

"Roger that, officer."

By now, the whole place is just toying with me. The senior executives are playing me like Dan Aykroyd got played in Trading Places. The more the situation devolved into chaos, I began to think that this was my vetting to see if I had what it took to be promoted to a corner office. I was like a pinball firing off the bumpers in a game called Company Party. Minutes ticked by, and the final inevitable move on the chessboard loomed. There were no other cards to play. It was either me or them, and I was pretty sure getting kicked out of the hotel in front of the boss's boss's boss would not be considered career positive.

The executives were locked in the party zone with the rockstar, and the rockstar was cranking up the crowd. Not only was the event not shutting down, it was getting wilder. That left me with one move. I had to become the bouncer. So, I just started grabbing people by the arm and showing them the door. I first looked for people I didn't know.

"Hi, Eric."

"Your name? Amy? Great. You work with Teva? No? You with Pfizer? Great. Get out. Thanks for coming."

Those were the easy ones.

One by one, the police officer just kept count as we sent men and women zigzagging down the hall toward the elevator. Once I cleaned out the competitors who were crashing our little bash, I was down to about five or six. Then it actually became a little fun. Suddenly, I was the kingmaker. I looked for people who I liked, and people who did good work or worked with us in marketing. They were safe. Any nurses were safe, as the whole thing was put on for them at the outset. It was suddenly my own little reality show, and I was Simon Cowell.

"Hi . . . Adam. Yeah, I love you brother, but it's time to pack it in. I'll see you in the office."

"What? Me?"

"Yeah, you."

When I had finally pushed about a dozen people out into the hallway, the long arm of the law was just about ready to relent, but he was having fun at this point, so why not push a little harder?

"One more," he said, almost smiling to put icing on his little game.

So, with one to go, I thought I would get bold. It was time to kick someone out who ranked above me. If the executives were paying any attention at all between drinks and rubbing shoulders with fame, I would look good pushing around someone ahead of me in the food chain. Company work is about chain of command, and the big boys had given me the reins on this situation and offered no help, so I thought it was a good move.

I surveyed the party and zeroed in on a director. My old boss, actually. This will be fun, I thought.

"Hi, Phil, looks like you've had a few beverages."

"Yeah, awesome night, Meyer. Boy, they got you running around like an idiot."

"Yes, they do, Phil. Time for you to take one for the team."

"Me?"

"Yeah, you. Sleep tight."

All told, I pulled it off. I felt like Chevy Chase standing in his driveway at the end of National Lampoon's Christmas Vacation, when he looks up at the sky and says to himself, "I did it." The cop left after shaking my hand and thanking me for the laughs. The after-party ended up migrating to the tour bus. Lots of people were AWOL to the convention floor the following day, and to this day, nobody has seen the drummer. It's always the drummer that goes off the rails. As my new police officer buddy walked off, he quipped, "Kid, you might be somebody yet. Keep it up. Tell the famous guy that trashing hotel rooms at corporate conventions is pretty lame."

"Thanks, officer."

* * *

Are there any lessons here? I think so, and it has to do with getting caught up in the moment. It has to do with seeing ourselves in the apostles. It has to do with humility when faced with the craziness of life. This was not a moment where I was forced to tackle deeply ethical decisions. It was not life or death. It was hardly even a consideration of right and wrong. I was an overpaid party planner. We were a little noisy, but nothing more sinister transpired than a bunch of overworked folks letting off a little steam. However, as I've thought about the situation over the years, it seems there is something to consider.

The characters at the party could have been playing a bigger role than we all realized in the moment. The rockstar was the guy everyone came to see. He was the one everyone wanted to be, but he was the only person in the room who could sing. People were so focused on him that they ignored all the other incredible skill in the room. Envy and jealousy are ridiculous distractions in that when we are consumed with wanting something more than our current station in life, we almost never stop to ask whether we are even qualified, capable, or willing to put in the time to achieve it. We just want the result.

In the case of Clay Walker, this guy is known as one of the hardest workers in country music. He works on his voice, constantly tours, keeps tabs on his business, and collaborates with writers. His band has been consistent and with him for twenty years, and he always, always is working the room for the next opportunity. Most people don't have that kind of energy when they are healthy and twenty-five years old, much less middle-aged with MS and having to compete daily with Zac Brown. Everyone wanted to be in the star's shoes that night, but most of us couldn't hack it.

To sum it up, the *Catechism* (CCC 1852) draws on the Letter to the Galatians to clearly lay out the effect jealousy and envy has on our odds of achieving the afterlife: "Now the works of the flesh are obvious: immorality, impurity, licentiousness, idolatry, sorcery, hatreds, rivalry, jealousy, outbursts of fury, acts of selfishness, dissensions, factions, occasions of envy, drinking bouts, orgies, and the like. I warn you, as I warned you before, that those who do such things will not inherit the kingdom of God." (Gal 5:19–21).

That passage reads like my punch list of shortcomings. All those items are on it, and I constantly fight these tendencies and inclinations. The Catechism hits hard on the temptations of the flesh, and our constant modern desire to try and keep up with the Joneses, or worse, our desire to be the Joneses is addressed with perfect clarity.

Next up, my friend the cop gives us a glimpse into morality. He just stood at the door, calmly directing and pushing toward the proper outcome. He was calm but resolute. It was late, we were noisy, and we needed to get a handle on the situation. Every time I came back with some modified version of the situation (enter sin), he just stayed on point. There was one solution that was acceptable. As I went back and forth in and out of the chaos, he actually became the one who was on my side in the situation. Think about that, the moral guideposts we bounce in and out of all the time are actually on our side in life.

I never got the police officer's name, but like all the other characters that I have run into over the years who are showing up in this book, he seemed to be there at a particular moment to make something obvious. In this case, he was our history, tradition, and theology in human form, simply standing at the door, calling for the correct outcome. Again, our proof source doesn't let us down: "What Christ entrusted to the apostles, they in turn handed on by their preaching and writing, under the inspiration of the Holy Spirit, to all generations, until Christ returns in glory." (CCC 96).

In layman's terms, I didn't really need my policeman buddy at the door to know the correct course of action for the moment. Nor did anyone else in that room. Deep down, we all knew that it was 2:00 a.m., and we were out of bounds. We knew right and wrong without needing to be told because the basic tenets of morality are always handed down generation to generation and will be until time ceases. No excuses.

My boss and all the executives in the room seemed to be acting in some small way as the Pharisees who show up in the New Testament. These are the guys who preside over all the rules of first-century Jewish law at the time of Jesus. They decide who's clean and unclean and who's worthy to enter the temple. They are the smartest guys in the room, and they call the shots. Plus, the Pharisees would not dirty their hands with the mess of life. They kept it highbrow and out of the rough and tumble of dealing with peasants and lepers.

That probably sounds like a stretch here, but my executive bosses were certainly holding court in the room that night, and the lowest guy on the ladder, who was not allowed into the tight conversation with their group, had to handle all the chaos. So perhaps it's a stretch, but nobody was coming down from that level to help.

Who was I at that moment? Maybe my character in that little single-act, late-night play was one of a confused apostle. If you read any of the Gospels, they are all ripe with moments where the apostles were bouncing between Jesus' mysterious teachings, the Romans, and the Pharisees. They were rarely sure of themselves. Time after time, they seemed to be acting on impulse and without much guidance or assistance.

For example, can you imagine what went through their heads when Jesus turned his new crew loose to feed five thousand people with a couple of fish and a loaf of Wonder bread? "The disciples said to him, 'Where could we ever get enough bread in this deserted place to satisfy such a crowd?'" (Matt 15:33).

The apostles were clueless while staring down five thousand hungry people.

"Uh, boss? You want us to do what?"

"Peter, trust me, just start passing out food."

"What am I gonna do when we're totally out after the first three people go through the line?"

"You are going to pass out food. Stay in the moment, and trust me."

"You're the boss."

In that case, they stayed in the moment and witnessed an event important enough for all Gospel writers to mention. When God repeats himself, we should listen. All I did was clear out a hotel bash at 2:00 a.m., and I certainly did not multiply the beers. But I did stay in the moment. The cop stuck with me. I didn't panic. He allowed me to work the problem until it was resolved. No doubt that's the lesson. God is always there. He's gonna stick it out with you if you stick it out with him.

Stay in the moment. You are there for a reason.

15

Fired and Faith

Some corporate guys have a gift. They say everything perfectly. You know this guy. He's polished, corporate, and climbing. In every meeting this guy attends, no matter the topic, he sounds like an expert. He's on. He's the corporate voice of reason as he interjects at the precise, correct moment while people sit up, drop their phones, and soak up his excellence.

Gimme a break.

This guy uses all the beautiful HR-vetted, appropriate language to weave a tapestry of points that always sound innovative and somehow never offend. The topic could traverse from brain science to quilting, and he's still the expert.

I don't trust these types of guys. Well, let's not be overly dramatic. It's unlikely he's going to steal my wallet or hit on my wife. Rather, I just don't trust that the overly calculated corporate guy will ever ultimately produce results, especially when the chips are down. This guy always hedges his bets.

Fired and Faith

This is where the case for faith in the corporate world really starts to get interesting. At some point, a corporation needs a few people who are willing to get dirty and turn over the tables in the conference room. We touched on this earlier. Corporations need a John the Baptist to stir things up a bit. Perfect, non-offensive corporate babble turns your company into milk toast over time.

Hopefully by these last chapters of this book, I've made the case for faith as a critical element of career and life. At some point, you must call balls and strikes, or your company and your family will dissolve into a meaningless cesspool of forced get-along in a world with no constructive conflict.

My corporate career has spanned the better part of two-and-a-half decades. During that time, I relocated my way around the pharmaceutical industry, pursuing marketing and field-leadership excellence.

The first company car, a brand-new Dodge Intrepid, showed up at the house in 1999. The company even paid for the gas. Employed fresh out of graduate school, I was on my way. My suit was sharp, and I rubbed elbows with doctors all day. The trunk was full of samples of allergy medication, brochures, and boxes and boxes of pharmaceutical pens.

Like all salespeople, I had a commission structure and all the perks. If I peddled enough medication, things were good. If not, my boss would fly in and have awkward, perfectly scripted conversations about performance, thus making my point from above. Why didn't he just call me and say, "Hey, you stunk last quarter, kick it up a notch."? I would have gotten the message loud and clear, and he could have saved himself the nights alone in the La Quinta motor lodge. Luckily, that only happened a few times, as I kept myself in the top tier of performers for two decades.

In all, I worked for three companies over about twenty-five years. I enjoyed my career and had no intention of early retirement. I worked my way up to leadership and built strong enough skills that employees followed me, stayed motivated, and gave me nice Christmas gifts.

"We make medicine, not machine guns," was my favorite line. I loved helping my people learn how to stand up for the good name of our medicines and the good name of our industry.

Like I said, I had no intention of leaving the industry which had afforded me a great career and a great family life. In early 2021, I had taken on an exciting role as regional sales director for a Boston-based company preparing to launch a new medication. It was awesome. As regional director, my job was to hire, train, and motivate a team of professionals to sell and represent the medication throughout Washington, Wyoming, Montana, Idaho, Utah, and Colorado.

In 2020, the COVID-19 pandemic was still in the middle of throwing a wrench in the world. All recruiting and staff selection was conducted via video conference. Training was also conducted via video, as well as all launch meetings and corporate updates. Months would pass before I would shake hands with my staff. Unprecedented it was, to say the least.

Back to my original point, stressful times require more than HR-filtered corporate speak. Stressful times require people to stand up, assume risk, and be counted. More on that in a few paragraphs.

The drug was launched about a year later. It was delayed due to an FDA advisory panel that voted nearly unanimously against approval, but somehow the company and the FDA managed to get it to the market. The press picked up on the story and never let it go. As a result of the controversy, Medicare was slow to pay, which made doctors uneasy to embrace the whole situation. Thus, the drug was very, very slow out of the gate, which elevated the blood pressure of the senior executives.

In most drug launches, a solid representative can make upward of $40,000 in bonus, and many win fancy awards trips to big resorts on beautiful beaches. Not in this case. The drug struggled, and the stock finished 2021 down nearly 40 percent. It was tough times in Boston conference rooms, but the bigger problem was (and still is) that there are millions of patients who finally had hope, left to only watch it dissolve into cynicism and chaos on the daily news. The whole thing was unfortunate for a lot of reasons.

All told, I lasted eighteen months. My direct reports did as well as they could. By the end of 2021, mine was the number-one sales team in the Western US and well in the top ten in the country. I'm proud of the work we did under extreme circumstances. The medication is complex and requires some upfront diagnostics that are also complicated. Further, the drug is administered by IV, so there were many details that had to be discussed before a patient was up and benefiting from the therapy.

Remember that 2021 was prime COVID-19 time, and as a result, my folks could not even get in the front door of 90 percent of their hospitals and clinics. Think about that for a moment. We were selling a product that was highly detail-oriented to customers who wouldn't use it until they understand those details, and the sales environment was in almost complete lockdown. Again, making the point above, there was no way to succeed in that environment while only using beautifully crafted corporate speak. Somebody had to hustle, work his way into uncomfortable situations, and make things happen. That's what my people did, and we finished number one. But on December 31, 2021, I was fired.

Let's get to the point now. I was eliminated in the middle of the vaccine mandate chaos. I was denied a religious exemption and given twenty-four hours to agree to the shot. That was a Friday. I was then unpaid on Monday morning, December 20, and fired officially on New Year's Eve. Just like that, my career was over.

Allow me to fill in a few more details that hopefully will convince the skeptics that I'm not a total fool. I contracted COVID-19 in spring of 2021. I felt a bit off my game for a few days. Shortly thereafter, I attended my long-scheduled annual physical, the joyous medical pokes and prods that all fifty-year-olds long for each year.

My labs came back normal with the addition that I carried antibodies for the virus. Following a cursory review at the report, I threw it in the file. It's important to note in the timeline here that in spring of 2021, the whole "vax" and "anti-vax" vitriol had not really ramped up yet in our national dialog. I didn't think much of it at the time.

Vaccine pressure ramped up globally in the late summer, early fall of 2021. My company issued a mandate with a November deadline. On that day, I submitted lab results with a note requesting consideration for exemption due to immunity. The note from my doctor specifically said that the vaccine is "not warranted." I was not trying to be a rebel. I was just following the doctor's orders and submitted the labs and the letter into the HR database.

Any logical person would conclude, as I did, that if any company would consider post-infection immunity as acceptable, it might be a giant, global biotech company whose business expertise is actually immunology.

Nope. Silence.

November came and went. December came, and the deadline for all employees to be either vaxed or exempt came and went with no acknowledgement of my status. To be clear, all I wanted was clarity on the immunity question before I made other decisions, but I received no communication at all until December 16.

I received a call from HR. They informed me that my immunity exemption was denied, and I had twenty-four hours to submit a religious exemption.

Now, it should be a dead giveaway that the guy writing a book on religion is at least somewhat religious by nature, so I confidently submitted my exemption request. In the back of my mind, however, I kept asking myself how a biotech company had any legitimate authority to make theological decisions about something as personal as one's faith.

Some companies in our industry were accepting any and all religious exemptions, while others were denying 100 percent of submissions. Not my company. They were accepting some and denying others. What?

The Associate Director of Diversity and Inclusion called to interview me about my faith. The first question was: "When did you come to your faith, and when did it become important?" I answered, "At my baptism as an infant."

That was a Thursday. On Friday, they responded with an email that stated my religious case wasn't strong enough to warrant exemption, and I had twenty-four hours to agree to get the shot. My boss called and said, "Tell them you'll get it." By that point, I just couldn't go any further. Tired, beat up, and unwilling to lie, I was shocked by the denied exemption on religious grounds. I'm no theologian, but I'm in the pew every Sunday, and I normally throw a couple shekels in the basket before grabbing free donuts at coffee hour. Shouldn't that have counted for something?

All told, HR was subjectively accepting and denying religious exemptions. Think about that for a moment and what that could mean in the long run. A mid-level HR associate, unschooled in theology, decided my religious acceptability. Under what authority can such a person, even if they consulted the legal department, make such a cataclysmic decision about something as personal and subjective as faith? Unreal.

To this day, there has been total silence from most of my colleagues and many of my friends. Nobody said much about the matter. My family didn't say much. A few conciliatory phone calls, but that's about it.

Back to the original point about the guy who speaks in beautiful, perfect corporate speak. Those are the guys who got us to this point. Those are the guys who silently sat in their gym shorts through eighteen months of Zoom calls while the pandemic slowly bled our culture of common sense. As someone trained in science, I hold no anti-vaccine or anti-science

Fired and Faith

position. But I am unapologetically in favor of honest discussion and individual autonomy.

For the better part of three years, corporate guys with all the perfect lingo sat on their mute button, seemingly unaware of the social meltdown happening in real time. They just kept on raising their Zoom hand at the safe moments in order to land two perfectly crafted and well-timed corporate answers per meeting month over month over month. These guys just pissed away three years during the most critical time in history, saying nothing of substance. And most of them were promoted.

The world doesn't need guys like that anymore. The world needs people who will go like Christ into the temple, turn over the tables of corruption, and make people notice.

What kind of world are we living in? You have more power to affect the answer to that question than you know.

*   *   *   *

This book has been about the collision of faith and career. It is a compilation of stories that transpired over the last twenty-plus years. I've been taking notes and writing blips and blurbs for decades. Each event caused me to think, in some small way, about faith and whether or not I'm just going to roll over and settle for the comfort of going through the motions. My prayer is that these chapters will cause a few good men to stop and think more deeply.

The unwritten expectation was always to be in the bar, drinking and entertaining the troops. Make no mistake, I was good at it, and I enjoyed it, too. On the flight home, I'd detox from the week and be ready to put on the Sunday face for Mass. It seemed impossible to be anything more than Jekyll and Hyde between work and faith.

What I didn't know all those years was that I was being prepared for a moment that would be unavoidable. No longer would I be able to keep my head down and pass by undetected. Faith would ultimately give me away and cost me my livelihood.

To be clear, I do not disparage or disrespect anybody who made a different decision than me in terms of the mandates. I simply could not get past the fact that a company had the audacity to turn HR and legal loose in choosing theological winners and losers. It's too dangerous to introduce such a practice into common culture. And it all happened while everyone seemingly just kept on repeating the same acceptable corporate phrases over and over on Zoom calls.

Exempt should be exempt. Period.

The result is I now know for sure that faith is everything to me. I tried to live in both the conference room and the church. I tried to keep them separated but know now such a life is folly. Corporations must be informed by honest, faithful people, or they will dissolve into chaos.

We must speak up.

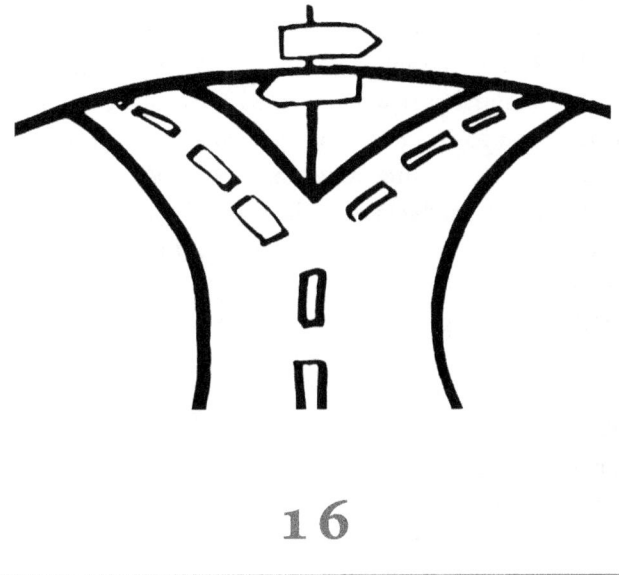

16

So What Now?

THE genesis of this little book originated from twenty years in the conference room and a million Sundays in church. I endeavored to tell some stories about corporate life that hopefully could correlate to faith. The Holy Spirit takes it from here. Perhaps these wandering memories will draw a few men like me back into a more active Catholic life. Being annoyed by the boss and pissed at ridiculous company initiatives is a constant struggle. It drives me nuts when I come home and the kids' backpacks and crap are thrown all over the kitchen table. Weaving a tapestry of profanity like that kid's old man in *A Christmas Story* is second nature. I've seen the bottom of thousands of beers in hotel bars all over the world. But I have never let go of my Catholic faith. Or more likely, it has never let go of me.

Matching up faith and career is no simple task. Everyone knows that "company talk" is normally pretty benign and that people sort of self-police, given that nobody wants to open a conversational can of worms with the militant vegan in shipping, much less a dialog on the theological proof of Christianity. However, it's worth noting that most of us believe in God. The guys that got famous with those What Color Is Your Parachute? books investigate this fact and make some very interesting points.

Richard N. Bolles, the author of the series, created the most successful career guidance manual ever written. In fact, it is flat out one of the most successful publications in history. While they are chalked full of career-building and career-rebuilding advice and guidance, Bolles and his team are not shy about faith. In the back of the book, there is an appendix section that is printed on light blue paper. That entire section is about faith at work. These guys are the real deal.

Evidently, according to data cited in the Parachute books, 89 percent of Americans believe in God, and the vast majority of those folks claim Christianity as their preferred flavor of religion. Their point is simple. People believe in God, so why are we all so quiet about it? It's worth noting here that anyone in the corporate world would immediately respond with the notion that speaking up on personal matters of religion could be a fast ticket to an awkward conversation with HR. But the point is worth considering. There are believers at work, so why not seek that oasis on the job?

Your job search and your work experience should have elements of faith interwoven into the process. God and faith are part of your makeup, and if your employer wants 100 percent of you, that shouldn't be a problem. If your worldview is influenced by Christ, your company is going to benefit from decisions made through that lens. As a hiring manager, I might want to know how you process information.

Imagine that conversation if it was allowed to actually happen in an interview.

Interviewer: "Mister Hitchens, tell me how you analyze information and what influences your decision-making process."
Candidate 1: "Sure. I'm and athiest. I make my own decisions based on a view of the world that I have created."
Interviewer: "Mister Aquinas, tell me how you analyze information and what influences your decision-making process."
Candidate 2: "I appreciate that question. Well, my worldview is informed by the Catholic Church, which has hundreds of saints, popes, martyrs, and great theological writers who for two thousand years have handed down the moral platform from which I process information and ultimately

make decisions. By standing on thousands of years of moral concrete, my decisions have the potential to truly benefit everyone."

Try that on in an interview, and you'll be back in the lobby, asking the receptionist to validate your parking in no time. But it is critical to have high-character professionals making sound decisions in all global corporations. Otherwise, our human tendency toward failure and corruption is only magnified. Remember Enron and our earlier discussion on the concept of concupiscence?

The Parachute guys go on, and it gets more interesting as they discuss how people search for fulfilling jobs. As job seekers, we tend to look for roles that match with what makes us enthusiastic. The ever-popular cultural phenomenon centered around "finding one's passion or mission" has made its way into the job market. Find what you are passionate about or what gets you excited, and make it your mission. The argument the "parachute" guys make is that this approach to fulfillment is too simplistic. Taking it further, one cannot separate passion or mission from religion and God.

In fact, the word enthusiasm itself is derived from the Greek words *en thous*, meaning "possessed by God, inspired." True passion is a gift from God, so if we seek a mission, we are ultimately seeking God. They sum it up perfectly: "The concept of Mission lands us inevitably in the lap of God."[1]

And then by deduction, God should end up in our careers.

* * *

My hope is that this book is an on-ramp for those who are willing to take another look, a deeper look, at the faith in which they were raised. It is my hope that somehow the interested reader will become more curious and subsequently begin to align faith and work into the same Christian worldview. Take God to work. Chapter by chapter, we have attempted to tell a corporate tale and then go a little deeper into the theology that is reflected in the story. If we're lucky, I've reintroduced a few folks to the depth, beauty, and historical resilience of Christ's little startup.

Full disclosure, and it should be obvious now, this is a quintessentially Catholic book. But make no mistake, it is written from an originalist perspective, meaning that the origins of Christianity are woven into our

---

1. Bolles, What Color Is Your Parachute?, 269.

Catholic documents. Thus, I hope the appeal of this book reaches across our Christian boundaries. Christ wants us to be united.

It's worth noting yet again that Jesus Christ was not born into high society. He had no financial backing nor the support of the occupying forces of the Roman Empire. The Jewish religion of the day was actively looking for the Messiah, but they missed 100 percent of the clues. They were looking for a great military leader who would come and claim Israel in the name of God. They completely missed the real point of Jesus' mission.

Jesus had no organization behind him. He was a carpenter from Nazareth. He was from the first-century equivalent of flyover country. Add to that, his followers were fisherman and tax collectors who also had minimal societal standing.

Jesus grabbed a dozen guys and started the job of introducing salvation to the world. Less than three years into his work, he was brutally crucified, and his followers scattered. It should have been the end of the story right at that moment. It should have been no different than Jim and Tammy Faye Bakker, who's ministerial fall from grace was legendary in the 1980s.

Jesus should have been just a blip on the historical screen. He was a dynamic, self-proclaimed prophet who lasted barely three years and was wiped out. But he is still here. He rose from the dead, literally. He now waits patiently for each and every one of us to return to the one who created us in his own likeness and image. His story endures. His impact on healing broken lives is undeniable. Just pay a visit to any twelve-step program. Christ is there.

The church Christ established has always been challenged by corruption, war, and division. The pews have always been filled with both saints and sinners. A scoundrel in the clergy is hardly a new phenomenon. Yet millions of believers continue to give their lives for the message, for the theology, for the truth. Regardless of the times our little startup church endures. Our Catholic faith rules. That's it. We rule. Suckers walk.

So, what's your move?

Appendix

You took the trouble to get to the end of this book. That means something. One of two things must be happening. One, you are curious and beginning to discern more from your faith, or you are on vacation, sharing a condo with the in-laws and picked up the only book on the nightstand to try and escape. Either way, I pray that God is using me, a most unusual servant, to help you get into gear. If you have read this book and felt the urge to go a little deeper, there are many options and a million starting points. If you are like me, you can't go from reading Dr. Seuss straight to understanding and analyzing the book of Revelation. Nor does it make sense to start going toe-to-toe with the guy in the front row of the church with the twenty-three Latin-speaking homeschooled kids. So, let's take it in four simple theological pieces. From there, you can run off and get your own PhD in divinity.

All Things Sex and Rock and Roll

Unfortunately in today's world, if you wear your Catholicism on your sleeve, there will come the day when you will be challenged on your archaic position on sexuality. For that reason, an explanation of church position belongs in this book. In ancient Rome, Christians were fed to the lions for simply believing. Now, it's more centered around being persecuted if you believe too much. The modern version of religion seems to be glossing over any and all tough theological subjects. However, on the topic of sexuality, it's best to think, pray, and discern the actual teachings so you can handle the challenge. You will be challenged, dismissed, and possibly shouted at, and that could all happen no further away than your family Thanksgiving dinner. The controversy surrounding sexual relationships is not going

Appendix

away, and a company man will sooner or later be required to attend the pride parade. So we better know the church's position on the matter.

My opinion is probably too simplistic, but I'll do my best. I don't hate anyone. Wait, that's not true, I would hate a person who sought to harm my family. Nobody has grounds to hate someone for how we may live. However, the problem is that the simplistic argument of "you're a homophobe" or "you're just a prude" does not allow intellectual room for an honest reflection on what our church is actually saying on these issues.

Modern society seems to have concluded that sexual gratification, in whatever flavor you prefer, is your right. You have the absolute right to sexual release anywhere, anytime, with anyone, without recourse. You want to watch pornos on the city bus, go for it. You want to hook up with fifty sorority girls, your fraternity brothers will salute you with high fives around the pool table. Society has granted us all the rights to eliminate any consequences, boundaries, or results of our sexual actions. In fact, secular culture would love to list "the right to sex" in the Bill of Rights just after the right to free speech and in place of the right to bear arms. We are told that anything goes. You be you. If we want it, we can have it: You want a woman, you want a man, you want to be a woman, you want to be a man—great. Heck, be a moose. Pick your bathroom. All good.

God has another thing to say on the matter, and ultimately, he makes the rules. God gives us much more to think about, and in no way is it about hate. God's position focuses on the goal and the outcome of sex, not the Hollywood photoshopped pleasure version. This is critical to the argument. The primary goal of sex is life; the bonus is pleasure. Thus, everything in romance and love, as far as the church is concerned, is focused on the primary goal of the action: new life. If life is not possible, the sexual contract is void.

Every issue of life and sex stems from that position. Marriage can only be with a woman and a man, not because they are in love and post cute photos on Facebook, but because they can make babies. No other definition is possible, as no other sexual combination can result in Junior Barnes the ten-pound toddler. There is nothing "hateful" about the church's teaching on sex. The doctrine is just crystal clear, unchanging, and unfortunately, it conflicts with relativism. The fire and rhetoric that surrounds the issue is missing the point. God makes his sexual teachings a matter of definition and logic, not a matter of emotion or feeling.

If you are the high school quarterback, she's cheer captain, and your love is hot like a Taylor Swift song, God won't endorse the sex. He won't

Appendix

endorse your love under the bleachers, not because he hates you, but because he loves you and wants you to have it all. He wants you to have the marriage, the trust, the sex, the pleasure, the baby, and the structure to support it all. You cannot build all that structure and long-term commitment in the back of your old man's Suburban. It's just not possible. So, sex and God start to look like more of a contractual arrangement than the love scene in an eighties romantic comedy.

Anybody with a job knows that you never get paid the bonus until the numbers are in and the money is in the bank. You never get an Olympic gold medal unless you dedicate, commit, do the work, and eventually win the race. You don't get the gold record unless you live in a van and play terrible gigs for twenty years, paying your dues. The same with the church's teaching on sex. The pleasure is a gift, but it is meant to be paid out as the bonus of the work and commitment.

He gave man and woman the responsibly of sex to bring life into the world. If we take on the responsibility, commitment, and openness to life, then our bonus is the occasional steamy Saturday night, complete with some Barry White music and a box of cheap chardonnay. Think about how powerful sex becomes when it's committed. Going further, we cannot make new life alone. We need a partner, but still, that's not enough. It's just sex, no matter who is doing it, until God shows up to conceive the baby. And he only wants to show up when the contract is signed and notarized. I'm trying to put common lingo on deep, deep theology. Sex is the only place where humanity actually physically participates in a divine miracle.

Whoa . . . so God set it all up for us to physically participate in a miracle?

If true, then trying to score chicks in a bar after ten beers quickly becomes pathetic. Sex without God is not how he defined it for humanity. And that's just it, God defines it and informs theology, not Cosmo Magazine. So, we're stuck trying to make sense of it all. When considering God's role in the issue, heterosexual, homosexual, or any other shape or form of sex simply doesn't exist in definable space, other than within the contract of a baby-making marriage. God does not provide any provision for the pleasure-only option. In this regard, gay and straight are all in the same boat. He only endorses the responsible, life-creating-pleasure option. He just doesn't define it any other way, and we can't change it.

The *Catechism* sums it up perfectly: "By safeguarding both these essential aspects, the unitive and the procreative, the conjugal act preserves

Appendix

in its fullness the sense of true mutual love and its orientation toward man's exalted vocation to parenthood." (CCC 2369).

There it is. "Unitive" is the pleasureful bonus of intimate connection, and "procreative" represents the baby. Both elements are essential. It doesn't mean God or the Catholic Church hates anyone.

Thus, I don't think we have to argue straight or gay in any of this topic. God set it up how he wants it. He wants married couples committed to the sanctity and creation of life. There is no theological right to sexual pleasure under any other definition. There is only the bonus of sexual pleasure if we accept the contract God outlines. That's it. We are not given the liberty to live one way on Sunday and do whatever we want the rest of the week. So, we either choose to align with God, or we align another way. We are free to make that choice. It's not a gay or straight argument. Rather, it is a question; it is God himself asking each of us, "Do you accept this mission?"

By rejecting the mission and vocation of marriage and redefining sex as some sort of exercise-like naked yoga session, we end up deviating from the original plan. Without God's contractual details, sex is then defined as whatever you want it to be, and the wheels tend to come off. When that train derails, we end up with frat bros with fifty partners, knocked-up cheerleaders, abortion, and wild experimentation; not to mention rape, incest, child predators, porn, and human trafficking. Liam Neeson would never have made the now famous movie *Taken*, had humanity kept us on the sexual rails.

If you don't accept the mission, it doesn't mean we are cast off and hated. Quite the opposite. It means we are choosing to go another way, and the door is always open should we want to return. The door is always open. God's invite to heaven is permanent. Our reaction to the invitation is up to the individual. The only permanence in sin is the choice to never return. The sin of separation from God is not a scarlet letter to be worn just by one group or another, rather it is an uncommitted sexual problem across the board. No marriage and no shot at a baby, then we're out of bounds. That's it. God set it all up and made his way crystal clear. Thus, as Catholics, we don't have to accept being called intolerant when we're all really in the same boat. God's position is clear from the very beginning:

> "That is why a man leaves his father and mother and clings to his wife, and the two of them become one body." —Genesis 2:24

Appendix

It ultimately comes down to the personal choice of accepting or rejecting the route God is offering. So, our choice is to join him or not.

Terrifying yet simple.

Christ Established the Church

It's a good idea to be confident that Christ established the Catholic Church. My take on it is that if God went to the trouble of sending his Son to die a wretched human death, then he must have had a point. He would have wanted that point to endure. Nobody wants to be a flash in the pan or a one-hit wonder, just ask Dexys Midnight Runners.

God knows full well the disaster that is humanity, so it's logical that he would have left the apostles with organization and structure; a leg up to get the process moving. What was it all for if Jesus was to ascend to heaven and leave us with nothing to help us triumph over the chaos of our own human failing?

The *Catechism* sums it up:

> "The Lord made Simon alone, whom he named Peter, the 'rock' of his Church. He gave him the keys of his Church and instituted him shepherd of the whole flock. 'The office of binding and loosing which was given to Peter was also assigned to the college of apostles united to its head.' This pastoral office of Peter and the other apostles belongs to the Church's very foundation and is continued by the bishops under the primacy of the Pope."[1]

The one power line in the Bible that sets up the organization of the church is found in the Gospel of Matthew. This is the moment when Jesus and the apostles are working their way through northern Palestine. They are in the city of Caesarea Philippi shortly after Jesus had fed the five thousand with two fish and bag of trail mix. Following the miracle of feeding thousands of people, the Pharisees show up, demanding a sign. "Who are you, really?" I sometimes imagine the main Pharisee acting like Tom Cruise in *A Few Good Men* trying to take down Jack Nicholson. Not in this case.

The scene in Matthew's Gospel then takes us to the power moment where Jesus asks his guys, "Who do you think I am?" Peter quickly answers and claims that Jesus is the Son of the Living God, which is where Peter comes to be the anointed leader of the church.

---

1 .*Catechism of the Catholic Church*, 881.

Appendix

"And so I say to you, you are Peter, and upon this rock I will build my church, and the gates of the netherworld shall not prevail against it. I will give you the keys to the kingdom of heaven. Whatever you bind on earth shall be bound in heaven; and whatever you loose on earth shall be loosed in heaven." (Matt 16:18-19).

That passage occurs right after the feeding of the four thousand and just before Jesus foretells his death. Thus, the moment is well timed for a business review. Peter is given the reins of the organization as well as the power to bind and loose on matters of faith, doctrine, and forgiveness. It is from this moment that Christ himself set in motion what would become the Catholic Church. It is also that exact moment that we can trace 266 popes in an unbroken line right back to Peter.

Therefore, when faced with questions along the lines of which church you attend, it is good to know that Matthew 16 is a good, high-level go-to proof source.

The Mass is Everything

It is also important to really understand the Mass. The Catholic liturgy is either a boring part of your Sunday where you struggle to stay awake, or it is the most awesome experience on the planet. There is no middle ground.

I experience the Mass in a particular way, and I have no idea if my viewpoint is unique. But for me, the Mass is the most peaceful moment I can achieve anywhere in my life. I experience all the same struggles I have dealt with forever; my mind wanders, I get bored, and I get groggy. But at some point in every Mass I attend, there is at least a moment that may only last for a couple seconds where I feel an overwhelming sense of peace and belonging.

Our Catholic Sunday ritual is everything. It contains the history, tradition, belief, Scripture, forgiveness, and spiritual nourishment we all need. The gates of heaven literally open up while legions of angels celebrate the greatness of God in the moment of the consecration. There is nothing like the Catholic Mass in the world. So, then why are 85 percent of us bored? For starters, I think we're just missing an important history lesson. I mean, Packers fans are easily able to sit on frozen benches in fifteen-degree weather when the team is 0–8. They can sit through a bad season because they have Lombardi and Favre in their memory. The history is the grounding

Appendix

that gets them through to the next winning season. We need to think of the Mass this way. History is on our side.

In order to take your faith to a deeper level, it is critical to figure out where the Mass came from in the first place. Saints have been martyred for the simple fact that they would not close their churches and cancel Mass. Monks have spent their entire lives writing about the presence of Christ in the Catholic liturgy. Why did these ancient thinkers and martyrs go to such trouble? What was the fuss all about?

The patristic era which stretched from the time of the apostles up through the eighth century is a brilliant time in church history, and some incredible documents survive to ground our faith and practice. The Didache is one such document, which in particular helps us understand the magnitude of the Mass. The Didache dates back to somewhere between the year 48 and 90. This document lines out the Jewish roots of the liturgy as well as the New Testament witness to the Eucharist.

The introduction of the Didache breaks it down: "On the Lord's own day, gather yourselves together and break bread and give thanks." (14:1).

So, this is where I start self-reflecting and saying to myself, "Uh, I've been sleeping through something we've done consistently for two thousand years."

The document continues to line out the Eucharistic prayers to be said over the bread and wine and then goes on to speak of the recommendation for confession before Communion: "First confess your sins, so that your sacrifice may be pure."

Boy, these early guys took this stuff seriously.

The story of the greatness of the Mass continues. Early in the second century, Saint Ignatius spoke of the Mass as a sacrifice. He referred to the real presence of Jesus as the Eucharist: "Take care, then, to have but one Eucharist. For there is one flesh of our Lord Jesus Christ, and one cup to show forth the unity of His blood; one altar; as there is one bishop, along with the presbytery and deacons, my fellow-servants."

Then by 155, Saint Justin brings the whole thing into focus and ultimately hands off the main elements of the Mass as we know them today.

Appendix

AD 155	Any Sunday in Detroit
On the day we call the day of the sun, all who dwell in the city or country gather in the same place.	Get your butt to Sunday Mass.
The memoirs of the apostles and the writings of the prophets are read as much as time permits.	Liturgy of the Word. Readings and the Gospel.
When the reader is finished, he who presides over those gathered admonishes and challenges them to imitate these beautiful things.	Homily. Wake up.
Then we all rise together and offer prayers for ourselves and for others, wherever they may be, so that we may be found righteous by our life and actions and faithful to the commandments, so as to obtain eternal salvation.	Prayers of the faithful.
When prayers are concluded, we exchange the kiss.	The sign of peace.
Then someone brings bread and a cup of water and wine mixed together to him who presides over the brethren.	Offering of the gifts.
He takes them and offers praise and glory to the Father of the universe, through the name of the Son and of the Holy Spirit, and for a considerable time he gives thanks that we have been judged worthy of these gifts.	The doxology.
When he has concluded the prayers and thanksgivings, all present give voice to an acclamation by saying: "Amen."	Great Amen.
When he who presides has given thanks and the people have responded, those whom we call deacons give to those present the "eucharisted" bread, wine, and water and take them to those who are absent.	Communion.

    Wow, we are participating in the very same ritual that has been practiced since Christ handed the reigns of the operation to the apostles! The Mass certainly has gone through changes, most notably when the Latin rite was replaced in most countries with Mass in the common language of the people. The big elements, however, are unchanged since 155 AD.

Appendix

The Eucharist Is Real

The last element a newly curious, faith-deepening Catholic needs to really digest is the concept that Christ is physically present in the bread and the wine at Communion. The big word for this is transubstantiation. The bread becomes the body of Christ, and the wine becomes his blood.

This is a tough one. The stats on the matter suggest that 85 percent of Catholics do not believe in the real presence of the Eucharist. Frankly, this shouldn't surprise anyone. We live in a world that downplays the mystical and attempts to only rely on the empirical. But in order to take faith to its full potential, this is perhaps the biggest hurdle for believers. The concept of the real presence of Christ in the Eucharist is spelled out all over the New Testament, but for our purposes here, we can illustrate the key sections from John's Gospel.

The scene is one as dramatic as only Jesus could set. He feeds five thousand people with a couple of fish on the shores of the Sea of Galilea, then he walks on water, to the utter astonishment of the apostles. Shortly thereafter, the group finds itself on the other side of the sea, and people start asking questions and asking him to show them more signs and wonders.

Jesus then launches into the most powerful statement on what we believe, and have carried forward for centuries, about the Eucharist. In John 6:22–66, Jesus explains clearly how he intends to feed us. He just fed five thousand and walked on water, and then he basically says, "You ain't seen nothin' yet."

> "Unless you eat the flesh of the Son of Man and drink his blood,
> you do not have life within you."—John 6:53

He restates this position multiple times and never stops to clarify or offer that he is speaking symbolically. It's not a warm teaching moment. It's not a parable with a life lesson. He is serious about feeding humanity with *himself*. His presence in us is what he offers. It's a tough one to grasp if, like me, most of your philosophical training comes from deciphering the riddles under beer caps. But he meant it. At the end of this dramatic moment, in verse 66, "Many [of] his disciples returned to their former way of life and no longer accompanied him."

Whoa. Jesus tells us to eat of his flesh and drink of his blood, then he doubles down for emphasis. Then a bunch of people stop following him because they don't get it. And the capper of the whole thing is he lets them leave. He lets them go. He doesn't attempt to explain it another way.

Appendix

We are free to go or to stay. But Christ is clear and steadfast in the message.

This is the whole enchilada on the Eucharist. Jesus, the new lamb, must be sacrificed. He makes it clear that many people won't get it, and they will leave the faith. The Catholic faith is hard. It is demanding. The Mass and the Eucharist are deeply theological and require prayer and dedicated discernment to understand. But thousands of years of church tradition, as well as Christ's own words, are all the sources we need to fully grasp this mystery.

Bibliography

Aquilina, Mike. *The Fathers of the Church*. Huntington, IN: Our Sunday Visitor, 2013.
Barron, Bishop Robert. *Catholicism: A Journey to the Heart of the Faith*. New York: Image, 2014.
Bill O'Reilly and Martin Dugard. *Killing Jesus: A History*. New York: Portland, OR: St. Martin's Griffin, 2017.
Bolles, Richard. *What Color Is Your Parachute?*. Berkeley, CA: Ten Speed, 2020.
Brian Butler and Jason & Crystalina Evert. *YOU. Life, Love, and the Theology of the Body*. West Chester, PA: Ascension, 2018.
Catechism of the Catholic Church Adult Studies. "History of the Catechism." https://www.catechism.ie/history-of-the-catechism/.
Catholic Answers, "Eastern Orthodoxy," https://www.catholic.com/tract/eastern-orthodoxy.
Catholic Biblical Association, translators. Holy Bible: Catholic Reader's Edition (NABRE). Wichita, KS: Saint Jerome, 2003.
Catholic Church. *Catechism of the Catholic Church: Second Edition*. New York: Doubleday, 2003.
Connell, Rev. Francis J. *Baltimore Catechism No. 3*. Front Royal, VA: Seton, 2012.
Dreher, Rod. *The Benedict Option*. Grantsburg, WI: Sentinel, 2017.
Durant, Will. *The Age of Faith: The Story of Civilization*. New York: Simon & Shuster, 1980.
Fulton J. Sheen and Morton, H. V. *This is Rome: A Pilgrimage in Words and Pictures*. Hawthorn, 1960.
Moczar, Diane. *Ten Dates Every Catholic Should Know*. Manchester, NH: Sophia Institute, 2006.
Pegis, Anton C. *Basic Writings of St. Thomas Aquinas*. Indianapolis: Hackett, 1997.
Pope Francis. "Feast of the Baptism of the Lord."
Pope John Paul II. "Apostolic Pilgrimage to Bangladesh, Singapore, Fiji Islands, New Zealand, Australia and Seychelles."
Sharpnack, Rayona. *Trade-Up! 5 Steps for Redesigning Your Leadership and Life from the Inside Out*. San Francisco, CA: Jossey-Bass, 2007.
United States Conference of Catholic Bishops. *US Catholic Catechism for Adults*. Washington, DC: USCCB, 2006.
University of St. Thomas. John A. Ryan Institute for Catholic Social Thought. Pontifical Council for Justice and Peace. "Vocation of the Business Leader: A Reflection." 2018.

About the Author

Eric Meyer is a twenty-year veteran of the corporate world who has found himself more and more curious about our Catholic faith. His stories are authentic, true, and simply reflect a lifetime in search of the truth. An experienced professional with global credentials in marketing, sales, and leadership make him unique to bring his Catholic perspective to the world. He lives in Moscow, Idaho, with his wife and four daughters.

www.ingramcontent.com/pod-product-compliance
Lightning Source LLC
Chambersburg PA
CBHW071440160426
43195CB00013B/1976